SUFISM

THE TRANSFORMATION

OF THE HEART

LLEWELLYN VAUGHAN-LEE

THE GOLDEN SUFI CENTER

First published in the United States in 1995 by
The Golden Sufi Center
P.O. Box 456, Point Reyes, California 94956

©1995, 2020 by The Golden Sufi Center

Sixth Printing, 2020.

Cover Illustration by Tennessee Dixon.
Printed and Bound in the USA by Sheridan, Inc.

ISBN 10: 0-9634574-4-6
ISBN 13: 978-0-9634574-4-8

Library of Congress Cataloging-in-Publication Data

Vaughan-Lee, Llewellyn.
  Sufism : the transformation of the heart / by Llewellyn
Vaughan-Lee.
      pages cm
  Includes bibliographical references and index.
  ISBN 978-0-9634574-4-8 (pbk. : alk. paper)
1. Sufism--Psychology. I. Title.
  BP189.65.P78V38 2012
  297.4--dc23
                                        2012003305

CONTENTS

PREFACE

Throughout this book, in an effort to maintain continuity and simplicity of text, the feminine pronoun is used for the seeker and the masculine pronoun is used for the teacher. Similarly, God, the Great Beloved, is referred to as He. Of course, the Absolute Truth is neither masculine nor feminine. As much as It has a divine masculine side, so It has an awe-inspiring feminine aspect.

In the end
a person tires of everything
except heart's desiring
soul's journeying.

Rûmî

INTRODUCTION

Sufism is truth without form.

Ibn El-Jalali

THE JOURNEY FROM SEPARATION TO UNION

Sufism is a mystical path of love in which God, or Truth, is experienced as the Beloved. The inner relationship of lover and Beloved is the core of the Sufi path. Through love the seeker is taken to God. The mystic seeks to realize Truth in this life and God reveals Himself within the hearts of those who love Him.

The mystical experience of God is a state of oneness with God. This *unio mystica* is the goal of the traveller, or wayfarer, on the mystical path. Within the heart, lover and Beloved unite in love's ecstasy. The wayfarer begins the journey with a longing for this state of oneness. The longing is born from the soul's memory that it has come from God. The soul *remembers* that its real Home is with God and awakens the seeker with this memory. The spiritual journey is a journey that takes us back Home, from separation to union. We have come from God and we return to God.

The mystical journey Home is a journey inward, to the very center of our being, where the Beloved is eternally present. He whom we seek is none other than our own eternal nature. Saint Augustine said, "Return within yourself, for in the inward man dwells Truth." The mystic experiences that the Beloved dwells within the mystic's heart, not as a concept but as a living reality.

In the depths of the heart there is no separation between the lover and the Beloved. Here we are eternally
united with God, and the mystical experience of union
is a revelation of what is always present.

The greatest obstacle that keeps us from experiencing this eternal state of union is the ego, our own
personal identity. In the state of union there is no ego.
In this moment the individual self ceases to exist and
only the Beloved exists. The Sufi says, "The Beloved is
living, the lover is dead." Thus the Sufi aspires to "die
before death," to transcend the personal self and experience our transcendent divine nature. The eleventh-
century Sufi, Ansârî, expressed this very simply:

> Know that when you learn to lose yourself, you
> will reach the Beloved. There is no other secret
> to be learnt, and more than that is not known
> to me.

The mystical journey leads us away from the ego
towards the Self, from separation back to union. Turning away from the ego and turning back to God, we are
led deep within ourself, to the innermost center of our
being, what the Sufis term the "heart of hearts." This is
an individual journey of the seeker back to the source,
of the "alone to the Alone." Yet there are stages on
this journey, "valleys of the quest," through which each
traveller passes. The Sufi masters have provided us with
a map describing these stages and also the difficulties
and dangers of the path. Having reached the goal, they
are able to help other wayfarers by recording what may
be expected along the way.

Sufism also provides certain techniques to open us
to the inner world and keep our attention focused on
our invisible goal. Foremost among these is the practice

of remembrance, for the Sufi aspires to remember God in every moment, with each and every breath. This is not a mental remembrance, but a remembrance of the heart, for it is the heart which holds the higher consciousness of the Self. The Self is the part of us which is never separate from God, and the consciousness of the Self is a quality of *knowing that we are one with God.* The practice of remembrance is a way of awakening the consciousness of the Self, and thus becoming aware of our inner union with Him whom we love.

If you love someone you always think of him, and when the soul's love for God is awakened within the heart, the lover's attention is turned towards the Beloved. The moment of spiritual awakening is *tauba,* "repentance," which the Sufis describe as "the turning of the heart." The moment of *tauba* is always an act of grace, a gift from the Beloved, but Sufism has developed techniques for keeping our attention on the soul's love for God, on the heart's remembrance. One of these techniques is the *dhikr,* the repetition of one of the names of God. Through the practice of the *dhikr* the attention of the lover is turned towards God and the whole being of the lover becomes permeated with the joy of remembering the Beloved.

The Sufi path helps to make us aware of the divine consciousness of the Self that is found within the heart, and at the same time guides us away from the limited consciousness of the ego. The journey from the ego to the Self is the eternal journey of the soul, of the exile returning Home. In this world we have forgotten our real nature and identify with the ego. The journey Home frees us from the grip of the ego and the illusory nature of its desires. We are led to the real fulfillment that can only come from knowing what we really are, tasting the truth of our divine essence. When one Sufi master,

Dhû'l-Nûn, was asked, "What is the end of the mystic?" he answered, "When he is as he was where he was before he was."[1]

Every spiritual path leads the sincere seeker to the truth that can only be found within. The Sufi says that there are as many roads to God as there are human beings, "as many as the breaths of the children of men." Because we are each individual and unique, the journey of discovering our real nature will be different for each of us. At the same time different spiritual paths are suited to different types of people. Sufism is suited to those who need to realize their relationship with God as a love affair, who need to be drawn by the thread of love and longing back to their Beloved.

THE ANCIENT WISDOM

Sufi is a name given to a band of mystics who are lovers of God. There is an ancient story about a group of lovers who were called "Kamal Posh" (blanket wearers), thought by some to be early Sufis. Their only individual possessions were their single blankets, which they wore during the day and wrapped around themselves at night. They went to every prophet. No one could satisfy them. Every prophet told them, do this or that, and they were not satisfied. One day Mohammed said that Kamal Posh men were coming and that they would arrive in so many days. They came on the day he said and, when they were with him, he only looked at them without speaking. They were completely satisfied. Why were they completely satisfied? Because he created love in their hearts. "When love is created what dissatisfaction can there be?"[2]

Sufism is the ancient wisdom of the heart. It is not limited by form, by time or place. It always was and it always will be. There will always be those who need to realize God as the Beloved. There will always be lovers of God. The Kamal Posh recognized that Mohammed knew the silent mysteries of love. They stayed with him and became assimilated into Islam.

Islam literally means "surrender" and, while the exoteric side of Islam teaches the outer religious law of surrender to God, there developed an inner esoteric side which teaches of the lover's surrender to the Beloved. A century after the death of the Prophet, small groups known as "Lovers of God" began to emerge throughout the Muslim world. They were also known as "Travellers" or "Wayfarers on the Mystical path," reflecting a saying ascribed to the Prophet:

> Be in this world as if you are a traveller, a passerby, with your clothes and shoes full of dust. Sometimes you sit under the shade of a tree, sometimes you walk in the desert. Be always a passerby, for this is not home.

Later these "Wayfarers" became known as Sufis, possibly referring to their white woolen garments (*sûf*), or as an indication of their purity of heart (*safâ*).

These small groups of Sufis gathered around their teacher, or *sheikh*. The inner teachings of the path are transmitted from teacher to disciple. Each teacher guides his disciples according to the principles he has received from his teacher. The essence of the teaching is not verbal, but a direct communion *from heart to heart*. The Kamal Posh stayed with Mohammed because he created love in their hearts, and it is the inner communion of the heart that is the core of the Sufi path. The relationship of lover and Beloved is reflected in the relationship with the teacher who guides his disciples, or *murîds*, with an openness of heart and an understanding of the mysteries of love.

At the core of all Sufi practices is the element of love and devotion. Devotion is the inner attitude of the lover, and the nature of the Sufi path is devotional. The Sufi aspires to give herself to God as a lover to her Beloved. Devotion is an opening of the heart to the grace that flows through love. It is an attitude of surrender in which the ego and the mind are surrendered to a mystery beyond their comprehension. In giving ourself to God we allow Him to take us Home, and the quickest way is through the door of love. In the words of al-Qushayrî, "The inner reality of love means that you give all of yourself to the One until nothing remains of you for you."[3]

It is said that there are two ways of attracting God's attention. Either we make ourself perfect and then He has to love us, or we give ourself to Him and then He cannot resist our need to be with Him. The attitude of devotion is an offering of our whole self to Him whom we love. This inner offering is a dynamic state of surrender which attracts the higher energies of love. Just as in nature a vacuum is always filled, so is the inner emptiness of surrender filled with His presence.

In the West we have tended to associate surrender with subservience and have lost touch with its hidden power. Surrender creates an empty space within the psyche which allows us to experience the power of the Self without being overwhelmed or inflated. Sufi practices are designed to help us to surrender, and to realize that we are contained by something far beyond the limited horizons of the mind and ego. Stepping into the inner spaces of our own being, we are able to experience the potency of His love for His servant.

Sufism has explored the ways of love and developed means to help the seeker travel this invisible and yet powerful path. Because the purpose of the path is to reveal the inner essence of the wayfarer, Sufism stays attuned to humanity. The deepest nature of mankind remains the same and yet surface changes take place. It is said that Sufism has stayed alive and preserved its dynamism through adapting and changing with the times and yet at the same time remaining true to the essence of the tradition. The essence of the tradition is the inner alignment of the heart towards God, and the surrender of the ego that allows His will to be done. But outwardly, as society and culture develop and change, so does Sufism respond to these changes.

EARLY SUFI SAINTS

Some early Sufis were extreme ascetics. Reacting against the growing luxury of life, they stressed the need to master physical desires. Even before the time of Mohammed there were among the Arab tribes men who had renounced the world, choosing poverty rather than riches. They believed that attachment to worldly goods and sensual desire leads to sin, and separation from them leads to the purification of the soul. These principles were carried into early Islamic thought. Abû Bakr, the first Caliph, preferred "voluntary poverty" to "compulsory poverty," and the second Caliph, 'Umar, practiced asceticism and austerity. For him seclusion led to freedom from evil.

Hasan of Basra was an influential early Sufi patriarch whose prescriptions for spiritual life were to sleep little, not complain of the heat or the cold, not have a fixed abode, and always be hungry. For Hasan, fasting was a "training ground" and he believed that fear should be stronger than hope, "For where hope is stronger than fear, the heart will rot."[4]

Râbi'a al-'Adawiyya, one of the foremost Sufi women saints, also lived in Basra. Râbi'a was an intoxicated lover of God who supposedly never had a teacher. She was an ascetic who used a broken pitcher for drinking and for her ablutions, an old reed-mat to lie on, and a brick for a pillow. Always looking towards God, she cared not for anything that might distract her attention from Him. Once Râbi'a was asked, "Do you love God?" She answered, "Yes." "Do you hate the devil?" She answered, "No, my love of God leaves me no time to hate the devil."[5]

Râbi'a became a model of selfless love for God. Nothing should come between her and her Beloved, and she longed for night so that they could be alone together. In contrast to the religious man who strives to reach paradise, Râbi'a's prayer emphasizes the mystical rejection of everything but God: "Oh Lord, whatever share of this world Thou dost bestow on me, bestow it on Thine enemies, and whatever share of the next world Thou dost give me, give it to Thy friends—Thou art enough for me."[6]

The ninth-century master Dhû'l-Nûn was one of the first Sufis to develop a theory of *fanâ* and *baqâ*, the annihilation of the self that leads to eternal life. He also introduced a theosophical doctrine of Sufism, speaking about *tawhîd*, or "Unity of God," and formulating a theory of *ma'rifa*, intuitive knowledge of God, or gnosis. The gnostic knows not through religious faith, learning, or discussion, but through being united with God:

The gnostics see without knowledge, without sight, without information received, and without observation, without description, without veiling and without veil. They are not themselves, but in so far as they exist at all they exist in God. Their movements are caused by God, and their words are the words of God which are uttered by their tongues, and their sight is the sight of God, which has entered into their eyes. So God Most High has said: "When I love a servant, I, the Lord, am his ear, so that he hears by Me, I am his eye, so that he sees by Me, and I am his tongue, so that he speaks by Me, and I am his hand, so that he takes by Me."[7]

Dhû'l-Nûn practiced self-mortification but knew of the supremacy of love. There is a legend that when he died there was seen written in green on his brow, "This is the friend of God. He died in the love of God. This is the slain of God by the sword of God."[8]

Most of the early Sufi saints regarded renunciation of everything other than God as the most important quality of the wayfarer. It was the great ninth-century mystic Bâyezîd Bistâmî who stressed that love for God is the primary means for realizing union, and preceding our love for God is His love for us:

At the beginning I was mistaken in four respects. I concerned myself to remember God, to know Him, to love Him, and to seek Him. When I had come to the end I saw that He had remembered me before I remembered Him, that His knowledge of me had preceded my knowledge of Him, that His love towards me had existed before my love to Him, and He had sought me before I sought Him.[9]

Although Bâyezîd recognizes the primacy of love, he also values renunciation. But rather than the renunciation of the world, he speaks of the renunciation of the self, the *nafs*. Pure love of God is only possible when one is free from the self. Bâyezîd says, "As I reached the state of proximity with God, He said, 'What dost thou desire?' I replied, 'I desire Thee.' He said, 'As long as there remains even one particle of Bâyêzidness in thee, that desire cannot be fulfilled.'"[10]

Bâyezîd was a God-intoxicated mystic who realized the essential unity of God and man: "I sloughed off my self as a snake sloughs off its skin. Then I looked into myself and saw that I am He."[11] He is known for his ecstatic utterances of divine union, "Glory be to me! How great is my glory!" and "Under my garments there is nothing but God."[12] He achieved this state of absolute oneness through severe self-mortification and austerity, purging himself of himself until nothing remained. Yet he realized that all his efforts must be renounced, for "through God's help alone, I attained God."[13]

In contrast to the ecstatic nature of Bâyezîd, the ninth-century master al-Junayd advocated a path of sobriety and the integration of Sufism into ordinary life. Al-Junayd lived in Baghdad, the religious and spiritual center of the time, and later Sufis were deeply influenced by his teachings on love, unification, and the surrender of individual will to the will of God. Al-Junayd stressed constant self-purification and struggle, which lead to the passing away of the attributes of the lover as "the qualities of the Beloved replace the qualities of the lover."[14] Al-Junayd describes how the stage of annihilation of the self, *fanâ*, leads to *baqâ*, the unitive life in God in which the devotee just fulfills the will of God: "It is a stage where the devotee has achieved the true realization of the Oneness of God in true proximity to Him. He is lost to sense and action because God fulfills in him what He hath willed of him."[15]

Al-Junayd knew of the dangers that can come from publicly speaking of the mysteries of the path, which are easily misunderstood, particularly by an Islamic orthodoxy which viewed the activities of the Sufis with growing suspicion. For this reason he rejected the "drunken" mystic, al-Hallâj, who openly expressed in the mosques and marketplace of Baghdad the secret of divine love, the essential unity of lover and Beloved:

I am He whom I love, and He whom I love is I.
We are two spirits dwelling in one body,
If thou seest me, thou seest Him;
And if thou seest Him, thou seest us both.

The themes of love, loss of self, and union were dramatically played out in the life of al-Hallâj. For al-Hallâj love was the very essence of God, "the essence of the divine essence." What separates us from Him is the self, the "I," which made al-Hallâj cry out:

Between me and You there lingers an "It is I"
which torments me....
Ah! Lift through mercy this "It is I" from
between us both![16]

The awareness that his own self was the cause of separation from the Beloved made al-Hallâj pray for his death so that that obstacle would be removed. Finally he realized his desire on the gallows, executed for proclaiming the mystical truth *anâ'l-Haqq* ("I am the

Absolute Truth"). Through his death, al-Hallâj became immortalized as the prince of lovers, as the one who was prepared to pay the ultimate price for love, his own blood.

Sufis have always been lovers, longing to return to their primordial state of union, knowing that it is their own self which is the veil of separation. They followed the Islamic law but inwardly their hearts opened to a truth beyond any form, to the limitless ocean of love. A lover cannot be confined or contained, except by the pain of separation; and the only rule of love is to give oneself to the Beloved. The sacrifice of oneself is the price that allows the devotee to realize God not as Lord, but as Beloved. Dhû'l-Nûn said, "O God! Publicly I call Thee 'My Lord,' but in solitude I call Thee 'O my Beloved.'"[17] Al-Hallâj's crime was to make this most intimate relationship public. His death made him love's martyr, and brought into popular consciousness the secret of the soul's love affair with God.

SUFISM AND THE RELIGIOUS LAW

Dhû'l-Nûn, like many early Sufi mystics, considered it necessary to follow the *sharî'a*, or Religious Law. He said that "The sign of the lover of God is to follow the Friend of God (the Prophet) in his manners, deeds, orders, and customs."[18] But the execution of al-Hallâj showed how Islamic orthodoxy was threatened by mysticism. Union with God cannot be reached either by the mind or by right behavior. God reveals Himself within the hearts of those who have sacrificed themselves on the altar of the heart; in the words of Dhû'l-Nûn, "He reveals Himself to them in a way in which He is not revealed to any man of the world."[19]

Although Sufism developed within Islam, its mystical wayfarers tread a path that can seem contrary to the outer law. For example, Abû Sa'îd ibn Abî'l-Khayr, the eleventh-century master of Mayhana, never went on the pilgrimage to Mecca, saying that the real pilgrimage was around the Kaaba of the heart. Abû Sa'îd ibn Abî'l-Khayr was a serious student of divinity until one day when, on his way to the city, he met a dervish seated on an ash heap, who introduced him to Sheikh Abû 'l-Fadl Hasan. The day after their meeting Abû Sa'îd was attending a lecture on the Qur'an when he heard the verse (6:91), "Say Allah! Then leave them to amuse themselves in their folly." The door of his heart opened, and when his Qur'anic teacher noticed this state he asked where he was the night before. Abû Sa'îd replied that he was with Sheikh Abû 'l-Fadl Hasan. His teacher ordered him to go to the sheikh, saying, "It is unlawful for you to come from Sufism to this discourse."

Abû Sa'îd returned to the sheikh, who recognized that he was drunk with divine intoxication. Abû Sa'îd had tasted the wine which devastates the mind with the mysteries of love. Wine is forbidden in Islam, but for the Sufi it is a symbol of mystical knowledge which is always forbidden to the rational mind. For Abû Sa'îd that sip of love's wine, which he said came from the glance of Sheikh Abû 'l-Fadl Hasan, made him abandon his religious studies and take up the mystical path. He became one of the great masters of Sufism, stressing the need to renounce the ego and cleanse the heart of desires. "If you wish that God should dwell in your heart, purify yourself from all save Him, for the King will not enter a house filled with stores and furniture, He will only enter a heart which is empty of all save Himself."[20] The negation of one's own self is combined with an affirmation of the heart's longing for God. It is through the spark of divine consciousness placed within the heart that the power of divine love is awakened, which opens the gate of unity. Then the negation of the self becomes a realization that "all is He, and all is by Him, and all is His."[21]

After his years of asceticism Abû Sa'îd reached illumination. He did not preach outward renunciation, but a participation in daily life together with absorption in God. For him:

> The perfect mystic is not an ecstatic devotee lost in contemplation of Oneness, nor a saintly recluse shunning all commerce with mankind, but "the true saint" goes in and out amongst the people and eats and sleeps with them and buys and sells in the market and marries and takes part in social intercourse, and never forgets God for a single moment.

Real poverty, say the Sufis, is the poverty of the heart, a state of inner detachment that does not depend on one's outer situation. Abû Sa'îd settled in Nîshâpûr, and, gathering disciples around him, he founded a *khânqâh*, or Sufi Center, where he was the first Sufi to draw up rules for communal life. Before his death in 1094 he asked to have inscribed on his tombstone, *Here lies one enthralled to love*.[22]

Another prominent Sufi whose path led him from theology to mysticism was Abû Hâmid al-Ghazzâlî. Al-Ghazzâlî was a successful professor in Baghdad at the end of the eleventh century. Unlike Abû Sa'îd's conversion from the glance of a sheikh, al-Ghazzâlî's began with the reading of Sufi books. But he plainly saw that these teachings cannot be learned from intellectual study:

… but can only be reached by immediate ecstasy and inward transformation. How great is the difference between knowing the definition, causes, and conditions of drunkenness and actually being drunk. The drunken man knows nothing about the definition and theory of drunkenness, but he is drunk; while the sober man, knowing the definition and the principles of drunkenness, is not drunk at all.[23]

Sufism is a path of inward experience, and as another great Sufi, Jâmî, said, "Why listen to secondhand reports when you can hear the Beloved speak Himself?" Al-Ghazzâlî gave himself to the mystical path and to the purification that transforms the soul and leads to secret communion with God:

Once I had been a slave: Lust was my master,
Lust then became my servant, I was free:
Leaving the haunts of men,
I sought Thy Presence,
Lonely, I found in Thee my company.[24]

But although al-Ghazzâlî's path led him from theology to Sufism, from mental knowledge to the experiences of the heart, his importance is in reconciling theology and mysticism. His greatest work, the *Ihyâ' 'ulûm ad-dîn*, "Revival of the Religious Sciences," contains forty chapters, forty being the number of days the dervish traditionally spends in seclusion at any one time. The *Ihyâ'* can be seen as a preparation for death, and the final chapter describes death both as the terrible moment that brings man to his eternal judgment, and the longed-for moment that fulfills the lover's deepest

longing and brings him into the presence of his Beloved. The previous chapters link these two threads
together, teaching man to live in accordance with the
inner meaning of the religious law, not just its outer
form.

Al-Ghazzâlî understood that "people oppose things
because they are ignorant of them." Through his work
he showed that Sufism is not antagonistic to Islamic
law, but rather that the Sufis follow its inner essence.
Combining the life of the heart with an adherence to
the law, his work helped to integrate Sufism into
mainstream Islamic thought.

IBN 'ARABÎ AND JALALUDDIN RÛMÎ

The early Sufi sheikhs often left no writings. Their
teaching was their own life, and although their sayings
were collected by their followers, there was no written
doctrine. Al-Ghazzâlî was one of the first to organize
his ideas into a mystical system. Half a century after
his death in 1111, one of the greatest exponents of Sufi
mystical theory, Ibn 'Arabî, was born in Spain.

Ibn 'Arabî is one of the few Sufis who did not have
a spiritual teacher, but instead was initiated, he said, by
Khidr, the archetypal Sufi figure who represents direct
revelation. Ibn 'Arabî left Spain in 1201 to make the
pilgrimage to Mecca, and then visited Baghdad before
settling in Damascus. He wrote a tremendous number of
works, perhaps five hundred. Many of them are short,
while *Al-futûhât al-makiyya*, "Meccan Revelations," has
five-hundred-and-sixty chapters.

The core of Ibn 'Arabî's mystical teaching is expressed by the term *wahdat al-wujûd*, unity of being.
Ibn 'Arabî replaced the idea of a personal God with a

philosophical concept of Oneness. Only God exists. He is the One underlying the many and is also the many. He is the cause of everything, the essence of everything, and the substance of everything:

> He is now as He was. He is the One without oneness and the Single without singleness.... He is the very existence of the First and the very existence of the Last, and the very existence of the Outward and the very existence of the Inward. So there is no first nor last, nor outward nor inward, except Him, without these becoming Him or His becoming them.... By Himself He sees Himself, and by Himself He knows Himself. None sees Him other than He, and none perceives Him other than He. His veil, that is phenomenal existence, is a part of His oneness.... There is no other and there is no existence other than He.[25]

Because there is no other than He, through knowing ourself we come to know God. "He who knows himself knows his Lord." This is not a philosophical concept but a mystical experience: "When the mystery—of realizing that the mystic is one with the divine—is revealed to you, you will understand that you are no other than God and that you have continued and will continue.... When you know yourself, your 'I-ness' vanishes and you know that you and God are one and the same."[26] *Fanâ*, the annihilation of the ego, one's "I-ness," is a state of realizing one's essential oneness with God. Nothing becomes God or even unites with God because everything is He.

What distinguishes man and God is that He is absolute while our being depends upon Him. Yet at the same time Ibn 'Arabî sees God and man as interdependent. Through our knowing God, God comes to know Himself. "God is necessary to us in order that we may exist, while we are necessary to Him in order that He may be manifested to Himself.... I give Him also life by knowing Him in my heart."[27]

The greatness of Ibn 'Arabî is not in the originality of his ideas. The theory of *wahdat al-wujûd*, unity of being, was already part of Sufi metaphysics. But Ibn 'Arabî formally organized ideas that until then had only been expressed orally. Later Sufis valued the work of "the greatest sheikh" for systematizing what they regarded as the real essence of Sufism. The unity which he describes is the unity which His lovers know within their hearts. Love's unity is beyond all form and embraces every form, as Ibn 'Arabî writes:

> My heart is open to all forms;
> it is a pasture for gazelles
> and a monastery for Christian monks
> a temple for idols and the
> Ka'bah of the pilgrim
> the tables of the Torah and
> the book of the Koran.
> Mine is the religion of Love
> Wherever His caravans
> turn, the religion of
> Love shall be my religion
> and my faith.[28]

Ibn 'Arabî became known as "the pole of knowledge." Four years after Ibn 'Arabî's death in 1240, a meeting took place that was to inspire some of the world's greatest writings on mystical love. A theology professor was walking home from school when he met

a ragged dervish. The professor was Jalâluddîn Rûmî
and the dervish, Shamsi Tabrîz. According to one story,
Rûmî fell at Shams' feet and renounced his religious
teaching after the dervish recited these verses from
Sanâ'î's *Diwân:*

> If knowledge does not liberate the self
>   from the self
> then ignorance is better than such
>   knowledge.[29]

Shamsi Tabrîz was the spark that ignited the fire of
divine love within Rûmî, who summed up his life in
the two lines:

> And the result is not more than these
>   three words:
> I burnt, and burnt, and burnt.

Shams had awakened in him a fire that could only be
satisfied with union, with the ecstatic loss of the self in
the presence of the Beloved. In his works he tells again
and again the story of love and death, how the lover
must die to reach his Beloved:

> I would love to kiss you
> *The price of kissing is your life*
> Now my love is running toward my life,
> Shouting, What a bargain, let's buy it.[30]

Rûmî and Shams became inseparable, lost to the
outer world in the love they experienced in each other's
company. For Rûmî, Shams was the divine sun that had
lighted up his life. But one day Shams disappeared,
possibly sensing the jealousy of Rûmî's students and

family. Rûmî was distraught, but then he heard news that Shams was in Damascus, and he sent his son, Sultân Walad, to bring him back. When Shams returned, Rûmî fell at his feet, and once more they became inseparable, such that "no one knew who was the lover and who was the beloved." But again the jealousy of Rûmî's students and his younger son destroyed their physical closeness. Again Shams disappeared, this time possibly murdered. Rûmî was consumed with grief, lost alone in the ocean of love.

But from the terrible pain of outer separation and loss was born an inner union as he found his Beloved within his own heart. Inwardly united with Shams, the theology professor was transformed into love's poet. Rûmî knew the pain of love and the deepest purpose of this fire within the heart, how it empties the human being and takes him Home:

> Oh, my everlasting heart! Toward the Beloved
> is a road coming from the soul.
> Oh, you who are lost! There is a path,
> secret but visible.
> Are the six directions erased? Don't worry:
> In the innermost of your being, there is a road
> to the Beloved.[31]

He had walked this road of annihilation, the sacrifice of the self that leads to union with the Beloved:

> At an end of "myself"
> He appears
> That Face
> Through these rags.[32]

Rûmî's greatest work is the *Mathnawî,* which Jâmî called "The Qur'an in Persian tongue." Its twenty-five-thousand verses are filled with stories and lyrics describing all aspects of the path of love, beginning with the song of the reed flute, the longing caused by its separation from the reed-bed. Including both sublime philosophy and the realities of everyday life, the *Mathnawî* gives a spiritual dimension to all aspects of life. For example, in the story of the chickpeas, the chickpeas complain of the heat of being cooked and try to jump out of the pot, making the housewife (who represents the spiritual guide) explain to them how through suffering one can evolve spiritually. In the middle of the housewife's story the chickpeas are taught to sing the words of al-Hallâj, "Kill me, O my trustworthy friends!"—the words of the lover who knows that only the "I" separates him from his Beloved.

If Ibn 'Arabî is known as "the pole of knowledge," Rûmî shines as love's pole. He radiated the light of love to the Persian-speaking world and beyond. And today the many translations of his work have brought his song of the soul's love for the Beloved to the Western world, introducing many seekers to the Sufi way.

SUFI ORDERS, TARÎQAS

Rûmî is known not only as a poet but as the founder of the Mevlevî Order, often known as the Whirling Dervishes on account of their mystical dancing. While the work of al-Ghazzâlî, Ibn 'Arabî, Rûmî, and others like Sanâ'î and 'Attâr established a literature for Sufism, the founding of the different Sufi orders, or *tarîqas,* was an important development in the practical application of Sufi teachings.

By the eleventh century the small groups that gathered around a particular teacher had begun to form into *tarîqas*, each one bearing the name of its initiator. The essence of each order is the tradition transmitted from teacher to disciple in an uninterrupted chain of transmission. Each *tarîqa* traces its chain of transmission through its founder back to the first Caliph, Abû Bakr, or the fourth Caliph, 'Alî. Different orders can be distinguished by the basic practices and principles which they inherit from their founder.

The first order to emerge was the Qâdiriyya, founded by 'Abd al-Qâdir al-Jîlânî (d. 1166) in Baghdad. 'Abd al-Qâdir was an ascetic, missionary, and preacher who became one of the most popular saints in the Islamic world, and his tomb in Baghdad is a place of pilgrimage. The Qâdiriyya is irreproachably orthodox. In the Arab West the order is called the *Jilâlah,* and its sacred dances have declined into trance dancing.

'Abdu'l-Qâhir Abû Najîb as-Suhrawardî (d. 1168) was the founder of the Suhrawardiyya. Suhrawardî was a disciple of Ahmad Ghazzâlî, younger brother of al-Ghazzâlî. Suhrawardî lived in seclusion and had many disciples, including his nephew Shihâbuddîn Abû Hafs 'Umar as-Suhrawardî, considered to be the real founder of the Suhrawardiyya. Abû Hafs 'Umar wrote an important and widely-read treatise on Sufi theory, *'Awârif al-ma'ârif.* His doctrine was both mystical and highly orthodox, and spread into India and Afghanistan.

At about the same time the Rifâ'iyya order was founded by Ahmad ar-Rifâ'î (d. 1178) and spread from Iraq through Egypt and Syria. Until the fifteenth century it was one of the most popular orders. The Rifâ'iyya dervishes were known as the Howling Dervishes because they practiced a loud *dhikr.* They also became notorious for unusual practices like eating snakes, cutting themselves with swords, and dancing in fire without being hurt.

In total contrast is the sobriety associated with the Naqshbandiyya, named after Bahâ ad-Dîn Naqshband (d. 1390), but started by 'Abdu'l-Khâliq Ghijduwânî (d. 1220). The Naqshbandis are known as the Silent Sufis because they practice a silent rather than vocal *dhikr.* They do not engage in *samâ'*, sacred music or dance, and do not dress differently from ordinary people. Another aspect of the Naqshbandi path is the *suhbat*, the close relationship of master and disciple. The order was very successful in Central Asia, and spread throughout India due to the work of Ahmad Sirhindî (d. 1624).

Another Sufi order, the Kubrâwiyya, was founded by Abû'l-Jannâb Ahmad Najm al-Dîn Kubrâ, killed in 1220 during the Mongol invasion of Central Asia. Najm al-Dîn Kubrâ's mystical theories concern visions and ecstatic experiences as well as a detailed color symbolism. His disciples had to follow a path which includes "constant ritual purity, constant fasting, constant silence, constant retreat, constant recollection of God, and constant direction of a sheikh who explains the directions of one's dreams and visions."[33] Bahâ'uddîn Walad, Rûmî's father, was one of his disciples, as was Farîd ud-Dîn 'Attâr, the author of *The Conference of the Birds.*

In addition to these Sufi orders there are many others, including the Chishtiyya, named after Mu'în ad-Dîn Muhammad Chishtî, a thirteenth-century Indian saint. Sacred music and dance are an important part of the Chishtiyya meetings. Among other Sufi orders are the Bektashiyya, noted for allowing men and women to meet together, the Khalvatiyya order, which believes in attaining spiritual perfection through seclusion, and Rûmî's Mevlevî order. There are also numerous branch orders.

Each Sufi path can be likened to a spoke of a wheel that leads from the rim, the religious law, to the hub, the heart of hearts, the Beloved. Each *tarîqa* has its own practices and principles to help us on this journey, to transform our physical, mental, psychological, and spiritual make-up so that we are able to experience the Truth that is within our own heart. We are guided by the sheikh, the representative of the tradition, and also by all those who have travelled this path before us, the superiors of the order, through whom the power and presence of the tradition is passed.

THE SPREAD OF SUFISM
AND ITS EMERGENCE IN THE WEST

Sufism participated in the spread of Islam, the orders adapting to the different peoples found in the Muslim world. Annemarie Schimmel describes how "large parts of India, Indonesia, and Black Africa were Islamized by Sufi preachers."[34] They spoke the local language rather than Arabic and lived out the basic obligations of Islam: simple love of, and trust in, God, and love of the Prophet and one's fellow creatures, without indulging in religious hairsplitting.

The different orders also adapted to the different social levels within Islam. In North Africa, dervish groups were an important focus for the spiritual life of the black slaves. In Turkey, the Whirling Dervishes were close to the rulers of the Ottoman empire, as well as being associated with artists and poets. In contrast, the Bektashi order was linked to rural, village life, while the Heddâwa, which claimed descent from the Qâdiriyya, was a beggars' order.

At the beginning of the twentieth century, Sufi groups could be found throughout the Islamic world, from Indonesia in the Far East to Bosnia in Europe. Then in some areas Sufism became suppressed, by Atatürk in Turkey (he banned the orders in 1925), by the communists in Russia, China, and more recently in Afghanistan, where Naqshbandis and their sheikhs were assassinated by Russian soldiers. But this century has also seen the spread of Sufism beyond the Islamic world into Western Europe and the United States.

While groups of Muslim immigrants undoubtedly brought Sufi mysticism into their Western communities, Hazrat Inayat Khan was one of the first Sufis to make Sufism accessible to the non-Muslim West. A sheikh of the Chishtiyya order, he founded the Sufi Order of the West, which stresses the universality at the heart of Sufi teachings. Other more orthodox Muslim Sufi teachers have come to the West, bringing the traditions of their order. For example, the Ni'matullâhî order, which was founded in the fourteenth century, was brought from Iran by Dr. Javad Nurbakhsh, while a Qâdiri sheikh from Ceylon, Bawa Muhaiyaddeen, attracted a devoted following in Philadelphia until his death in 1986.

The different Sufi orders that have arrived in the West have increased interest in the teachings of the Sufi tradition. At the same time, translations of Sufi texts from Arabic and Persian have made its literature more accessible. Integrating Sufi ideas into Western thought has also been helped by the scholarly work of Henry Corbin, who offers a psychological perspective on the theories of Ibn 'Arabî, Suhrawardî, Najm al-Dîn Kubrâ, and others. Corbin was also a follower of Carl Jung and showed how Jung's understanding of the archetypal world of the collective unconscious is mirrored in Sufism. Corbin's work has been very influential in certain schools of Jungian psychology, in particular the work of James Hillman and his school of "Archetypal Psychology."

Idries Shah, associated with the Naqshbandiyya in Afghanistan, also offers a psychological approach to Sufism. He suggests that Sufi literature speaks about psychological states and processes that we are only just beginning to understand in the West. Translating many Sufi stories into English for the first time, he has brought us the teachings and humor of this mystical tradition, including the exploits of Mullâh Nasruddîn. Nasruddîn's folk wisdom is often very applicable today. The story of the Mullâh searching the ground in front of his hut speaks directly to our Western, rational approach to many of our problems. When a passerby saw Nasruddîn bending in the dust and asked him what he was doing, Nasruddîn replied that he was looking for a lost key. The passerby offered to help him look. After fruitlessly searching for some time, the helper asked Nasruddîn where exactly he had lost the key, to which the Mullâh replied, "In my hut."

"Then why are you looking for it out here?"

"Because out here is more light."

TRUTH BEYOND FORM

Whatever form Sufism takes, simple or scholarly, orthodox or universal, it speaks of a truth that is beyond any form. Rûmî says this clearly in the story of Moses and the shepherd. After Moses criticizes a shepherd for praying to God in his own simple language and not using the appropriate terms, God rebukes him, saying:

"I have given each being a separate and
  unique way
of seeing and knowing and saying that
  knowledge.
What seems wrong to you is right for him.
What is poison to one is honey to someone else....
  Hindus do Hindu things.
The Dravidian Muslims in India do what they do.
It's all praise, and it's all right....
  Moses
those who pay attention to ways of behaving
and speaking are one sort.
  Lovers who burn are another." [35]

For lovers of God there are no rules for worship. "The Love-Religion has no code or doctrine. Only God."[36] As Moses finally tells the shepherd, "Say whatever and however your loving tells you." The real prayer of the Sufi is beyond words, a merging of the heart of the lover into the heart of the Beloved.

Sufism responds to the need of the time and the place and the people. As a bridge from the world of forms to the formless it needs on the outside to have a particular form, but inwardly each path is about the burning, melting, and merging of the lover in the fire of love's longing and devotion. He, the Great Beloved, ignites the spark of desire within the heart of His servant, and then guides us to the path that will take us Home, the path that is most suited to our individual nature and will therefore take us Home the quickest. Some souls need music and dance to awaken the remembrance of the heart. For others, silence is the only way.

Sufis are unattached to ways or means because the only attachment of the lover is to the Beloved. These wayfarers know that the ego is the one real obstacle on the path and in their hearts call out the words of a Sufi prayer:

> May God empty my very self
> Of all except His own presence.

The "death" of the ego is the transformation of the heart that takes place on the path of love. Only when the ego has surrendered itself on the altar of love can the lover and Beloved unite. But we cannot do this work alone for the simple reason that the ego cannot transcend itself just as the mind cannot go beyond the mind. The wisdom of past masters and the practices and principles of the path help us, together with the guidance of the sheikh. But of greatest importance is the way the path opens us to the grace of God, without which all our efforts would be useless. It is only the Beloved who can take the lover from separation back to union. In the words of Kalâbâdhî, "The only guide to God is God Himself."

1. THE LONGING OF THE HEART

If the eight Paradises were opened in my hut,
and the rule of both worlds were given in my hands,
I would not give for them that single sigh which rises
at morning-time from the depth of my soul
in remembering my longing for Him.

Bâyezîd Bistâmî[1]

AWAKENING TO THE PAIN OF SEPARATION

The journey back to God begins when He looks into the heart of His servant and infuses it with divine love. This is the moment of *tauba*, "the turning of the heart." The glance of the Beloved awakens the memory of the soul, the memory of our primordial state of oneness with God. The memory of this union makes us aware that we are now separate from the One we love, and so ignites the fire of longing. The exile remembers his real Home and begins the long and lonely journey back to the Beloved.

Without the glance of the Beloved there would be no longing for God and no spiritual journey. It is only because He wants us that we turn away from the outer world and set out on the ancient journey of the soul back to its source. Someone once asked Râbi'a, "I have committed many sins; if I turn in penitence towards God, will He turn in mercy towards me?" "Nay," she replied, "but if He shall turn towards thee, thou wilt turn towards Him."

The moment of *tauba* can be the glance of a teacher, as when Rûmî fell at the feet of Shams. It is rarely so outwardly dramatic, but the presence of someone who is spiritually awake can trigger a response of the heart, bringing into consciousness a hidden homesickness for one's real Home. Then in an instant the inner orientation of the individual changes. A doorway to the beyond has been opened, through which we glimpse the soul's deepest desire. Once this desire is awakened we are left with a sweet and terrible longing for what we have seen:

> The world is full of beautiful things until an old man with a beard came into my life and set my heart aflame with longing and made it pregnant with Love. How can I look at the loveliness around me, how can I see it, if it hides the Face of my Lover?[2]

For some their longing is awakened by a teacher, while others may be awakened by a dream, a saying, or a piece of music that strikes the heart's primal chord. It may be a moment in nature when, for an instant, the door between the two worlds opens, or even a shock that momentarily frees us from the grip of the ego and the mind. In whatever way the Beloved wills, He comes to us, for this longing is always a gift of God, sent to the exile inviting him to set out Home.

The awakening of longing is the initial awakening of the heart. We hear His call not with the outer ear but with the ear of the heart. This call is always present because each and every atom sings the song of remembrance, every particle of creation desires to be reunited with the Creator. His call is at the core of creation; without it the world would disintegrate. It is the centripetal pull which balances the centrifugal, expansive energy of creation. We feel this inner gravitational pull towards God as the magnetic attraction of love, which is experienced as a desire for closeness and intimacy. Love always draws us closer and closer towards union.

Love's call is at the very center of our being and we experience it reflected in human relationships. But we are not aware of its deepest purpose, we cannot hear its real message, until the heart is awakened:

> Know that all will return to its origin. The heart, the essence, has to be awakened, made alive, to find its way back to its divine origin.[3]

DIVINE DISCONTENT

For some seekers this initial awakening is experienced as a growing feeling of dissatisfaction, what Saint Augustine called "the Divine Discontent." In the innermost chamber of the heart we have seen His face but this is hidden from consciousness. The heart speaks a language so different from that of the mind and the ego that we are not directly aware of what has happened. Instead we are left with a feeling of the emptiness of our ordinary life. The painful side of spiritual awakening is that the world becomes desolate. We may try to improve our outer situation, work harder, make money, or take a vacation. But we soon find that this is no answer. What is it that we really want? Why is the outer world losing its attraction? Friends and interests that used to be fulfilling can seem empty, and we are left only with a discontent that we cannot satisfy.

We long for what our heart knows to be real, for love's union which is hidden beneath the surface of our lives. When we are awakened to this real love we can never be satisfied by anything else. This is why the world begins to lose its attraction, why we become discontented. We have been given a glimpse of something else, the real substance of our own self. Longing is both a blessing and a curse. A blessing because it takes us Home, and a curse because of the pain it brings. Nothing can satisfy us but union with God. Râbi'a, who knew the deepest meaning of love's pain, expresses this in her usual straightforward way:

> The source of my grief and loneliness is deep
>   in my breast.
> This is a disease no doctor can cure.
> Only union with the Friend can cure it.[4]

THE CRY OF THE SOUL

Within the heart, a sadness has been awakened that can never be healed by the outer world or the most meaningful human relationship. The soul begins to cry the primal cry of separation, the heart's longing for God. This is the song of the reed flute at the beginning of Rûmî's *Mathnawî*:

> Listen to the reed how it tells a tale,
>   complaining of separations,
> Saying, "Ever since I was parted from the reed-
>   bed, my lament has caused man and woman
>   to moan.
> It is only to a bosom torn by severance that I
>   can unfold the pain of love-desire.
> Everyone who is left far from his source
>   wishes back the time when he was united
>   with it."[5]

This pain of longing is the most direct road back to God. Longing does not belong to the complexities of the mind or the veils of the ego. Within the heart the Beloved speaks directly to the lover, leading us through the fire of our own transformation. If we follow the thread of longing we step out of the ego, with its patterns of control, and enter the arena of the heart. It is the heart that hears His call:

> Know that you are the veil which conceals yourself from you. Know also that you cannot reach God through yourself, but that you reach Him through Him. The reason is that when God vouchsafes the vision of reaching Him, He calls upon you to seek after Him and you do.[6]

He calls us to Him with the irresistible attraction of love, which we experience as longing. In order to fully hear His call we have to allow ourself to be dissatisfied and unfulfilled, rather than trying to fill this painful vacuum with another distraction. We have to allow the pain of longing into our life. Longing is both the pain that burns away the veils of separation and the thread that guides us deeper and deeper within, until we are able to enter the innermost chamber of the heart where He is waiting.

In the West we are conditioned to believe that at the beginning of every journey we should know where we are going and how to get there. Caught in this conditioning, we apply it to spiritual life: what is the goal we seek and what are the practices that will take us there? But the real journey of the soul is not of our own choosing, nor can we find our own way. We are responding to a call that will take us beyond the known into the unknown, beyond the world of forms into the formless.

The spiritual journey is the most difficult undertaking. It is a voluntary crucifixion in which we die to the ego. Of our own accord we would never turn away from the world with its many attractions and illusions and begin this painful, lonely quest. It is only because He calls us, because He attracts our attention with His love, that we set out upon the path of no return. Like a magnet He draws us to Him with love, for, in the words of the Sufi poet Nizâmî, "If the magnet were not loving, how could it attract the iron with such longing?"[7]

THE KNOWLEDGE OF UNION

The irresistible nature of His love is that it has the quality of completeness. All human love is incomplete, never totally fulfilling. But His love carries the song of union, the total oneness of lover and Beloved. This is what we knew before separation, before we were sent as exiles into this world. Within the innermost core of the human being there is a place where we remain one with God. The Sufis call this place the heart of hearts. It is the home of the Self, our divine consciousness. The Self is the part of us that is *never separate from God.* We carry this state of oneness within us and yet we have forgotten it. His love awakens us to its eternal presence.

He for whom we long is so close to us and yet we cannot see Him. He is "nearer to you than your very neck vein," and yet we cannot touch Him. In Rûmî's words, "You guard the treasury of God's Light—so come, return to the root of the root of your own self!"[8] The longest and most painful journey is the journey back to ourselves. Longing is our guide. It is the pull of His love that takes us through the darkness of separation. Longing keeps our attention on the heart and keeps alive the memory of our real nature.

The greater the longing the greater the attraction of the Beloved. This is why the Sufi prays, "Give me the pain of love, the pain of love for Thee! And I will pay the price, any price you ask!"[9] The pain of love is the knowledge that we are separate from the one we love. This is not a mental knowledge but a knowledge of the soul which we feel in the heart. The soul knows the truth of love: that we belong to the Beloved. The soul has tasted the wine of union, "has drunk the wine before the creation of the vine."[10] Before we come into this world we are with God.

The knowledge of union evokes the pain of separation. Only because we remember that we are one with God do we experience this state of separation. But unlike the memories of the mind, this memory of the heart does not belong to time. What we remember is the *eternal moment of the soul when we are always united with God.* The remembrance of the heart is an awareness of a different level of reality where there is no duality and no time. In the depths of the heart the lover and the Beloved are eternally united, and in everyday consciousness there is always separation. Love's most painful paradox which consumes the lover with longing is that we are both united and separate.

He awakens us to the eternal moment of union and the weary hours of separation. In the state of separation, longing draws us into the heart. Longing is both the call and the path we follow. His imprint is the sigh of the soul. When we give ourself to this primal pain we walk in His footsteps to Him:

> By his own powers no one can find the
>   way that leads to Him;
> Whoever walks towards Him walks with
>   *His* foot.

Until the beam of His love shines out to guide
the soul,
It does not set out to behold the love of
His face.
My heart feels not the slightest attraction
towards Him
Until an attraction comes from Him and works
upon my heart.
Since I learnt that He longs for me, longing for
Him never leaves me for an instant.[11]

THE LIMITLESS OCEAN OF LONGING

Longing can take many different forms. For some it
comes like a physical pain within the heart. For others
it is a dull ache beneath the surface of their lives, a
hidden grief, an unexplained sadness. Depending on its
intensity it can cause overwhelming despair or a nagging
discontent. It can appear unexpectedly, bursting into
consciousness with the pain of lost love, and then melt
away, leaving an unexplained sweetness or the exhaus-
tion of spent passion. But deep within us this grief
is always present, for it is the soul's remembrance of
union. In the words of Meister Eckhart, "God is the sigh
in the soul."

Sometimes we can embrace this longing and welcome it into our lives. We recognize how precious is
this pain. But the heart's longing can also be terrifying,
making us run and hide in the distractions of the outer
world. We cannot contain or control this sadness. Nor
can we rationally understand its purpose, for it draws
us into a journey beyond any known horizon. Longing
is as limitless as love's ocean. It has no end because
love has no end. Dhû'l-Nûn tells a story of meeting a

woman on the seashore who revealed to him the mysteries of the path. He asked her, "What is the end of love?"and she answered, "O simpleton, love has no end." He asked, "Why?" She replied, "Because the Beloved has no end."[12]

Longing is without end because love is without end. Love and longing do not belong to the dimension of time or space, but to the infinite dimension of the Self. To be confronted by an endless ocean of grief is terrible. This is not an ocean we can cross, because, in Rûmî's words, this is "the shoreless sea; here swimming ends always in drowning."[13] Only through dying to the ego can we merge into the infinite ocean of the Self. Confronted by the heart's unspoken ultimatum, how often do we run away from the sea's edge back into the complexities of the mind and the many illusions of the outer world?

> I fled Him, down the nights and down the days;
> I fled Him down the arches of the years;
> I fled Him down the labyrinthine ways
> Of my own mind; and in the midst of tears
> I hid from Him, and under running laughter ...[14]

But once longing is awakened within the heart we can never escape it. However far we run it will always haunt us as a lover whom we have betrayed. Whatever our seeming achievements, life will have a sour note of deep disappointment. The poet who flees Him hears His feet following, and hears His voice saying, "All things betray thee, who betrayest Me."

Longing is the grief that consumes the ego. Longing is intimate, endless, tortuous, and terrible. It is the pain that underlies every heartache, every feeling of loss. If we feel rejected or abandoned by a parent, friend, or human lover, at the core of this feeling is the primal pain of separation from God. He with whom we were united betrayed us and banished us from paradise. From the state of union we were sent as exiles into this world of separation. Mankind's crucifixion is to be both human and divine—the soul which has tasted union imprisoned in a world of duality. Christ's cry on the cross, "My God, my God, why hast Thou forsaken me?"[15] echoes deep within the heart of each of us. To embrace the pain of longing is to make conscious the deepest grief of humanity.

Nothing is more painful than to consciously feel within our own heart that we are separate from God. On the level of the soul all humanity knows this separation but it is hidden from consciousness. Only when we know that we are contained within His love can we bear the real intensity of this experience. In the moment of *tauba*, when He gives our heart a glimpse of unity, the knowledge of *His love for us* is imprinted upon the heart. This imprint allows us to consciously experience the intensity of separation. The momentary experience of union both awakens the pain of separation and enables us to contain the pain.

The knowledge imprinted on the heart is not the same as mental knowledge. The knowledge of the heart is both more certain and more elusive: more elusive because it is far finer and more difficult to grasp than the mind's thought-forms; more certain because it is not relative, but belongs to the absolute world of the Self. As we travel along the path we hear more clearly the wisdom of the heart and can distinguish its voice from the mind and the ego. But from the very beginning this inner certainty is present. The heart knows that we are held within the circle of love.

THE FEMININE SIDE OF LOVE

Love comes from the beyond and is our direct link with God. But like everything that is a part of creation, love has a dual nature, a positive and negative, masculine and feminine aspect. The masculine side of love is "I love you." Love's feminine aspect is "I am waiting for you. I am longing for you." The feminine side of love is the cup waiting to be filled, the heart longing for the wine of divine intoxication.

The lover waits for the Beloved, the soul waits for God. The mystery of the soul's feminine nature is one of love's secrets. The sixteenth-century Indian princess and poet, Mirabai, knew this. Once, because she was a woman, she was denied access to one of Krishna's temples by a famous theologian and ascetic, Jiv Gosvami. She shamed him with the words, "Are not all souls feminine before God?" He bowed his head and led her into the temple.[16] *The Song of Songs* also celebrates the soul's feminine relationship to God in mystical symbolism filled with sensuality:

> I sleep but my heart waketh: it is the voice of my Beloved that knocketh, saying, "Open to me, my sister, my love, my dove, my undefiled: for my head is filled with dew, and my locks with the drops of the night...."
>
> I rose up to open to my Beloved; and my hands dropped with myrrh, and my fingers with sweet-smelling myrrh, upon the handles of the lock.[17]

The soul waits and opens to the Beloved, just as the heart waits and then opens to the tenderness of His touch, to the infusion of His love. *The Song of Songs* is one of the most beautiful evocations of the mystical love of the soul for God, and yet, like many aspects of the feminine, it has been misunderstood and repressed by our patriarchal culture. The Church fathers could not deny that the *Song of Songs* belonged in the Bible, but they tried to interpret this erotic and mystical poem as the relationship between Mother Church and Christ. Those who have tasted just for an instant the inner relationship with the Beloved can hear instead the depth and passion of the receptive soul that waits for the intoxicating embrace of her divine Lover.

Gradually we have become aware of our culture's patriarchal injustice towards women. We are far less aware of our denial and repression of the inner feminine. As a culture we need to rediscover and value many feminine qualities, such as *being* rather than *doing; relating, allowing,* and *listening; creating space* rather than *creating form.* Many of these qualities are essential to the mystic, who needs to rediscover her own natural way of being with God, create a sacred space for this meeting, learn to listen to His silent voice, and allow Him into her life.

The mystical path is in essence a feminine path of surrender and devotion, as expressed in a simple Sufi prayer:

> I offer to Thee the only thing I have:
> My capacity of being filled with Thee.

The mystic gives herself to her Beloved and so allows Him to come into her and dissolve all traces of duality. Longing is a dynamic state of waiting in which the soul offers herself to God, and it is the very core of the mystical path. The anonymous author of the fourteenth-century Christian classic, *The Cloud of Unknowing,* says that "Your whole life must be one of longing." Yet many people have an instinctual longing, a homesickness of the soul, but do not know it. Instead they interpret this feeling as a failing, an inability to be happy or fulfilled with what life offers. Longing can so easily be misunderstood as a psychological problem, even a depression. One who suffers it can feel rejected and isolated, not realizing that longing is the greatest gift because it does not allow us to forget Him whom the heart loves.

We need to reclaim the potency of longing, to value its spiritual power. Rather than denying our longing we should welcome it and pray for it to increase. Longing is the remembrance of the heart that both guides and nourishes the wayfarer. Ibn 'Arabî prayed "Oh Lord, nourish me not with love but with the desire for love."[18]

Longing is a *direct connection* from the heart of the seeker to the heart of the Beloved. Longing is not entangled within the psyche in our complexes and patterns of conditioning; nor does it function on the level of the mind where it can be strangled by doubts. Longing is a living prayer of love. In the words of the eleventh-century Sufi, al-Qushayrî, "Longing is a state of commotion in the heart hoping for meeting with the Beloved. The depth of longing is commensurate with the servant's love of God."[19]

CONFRONTING THE DENIAL OF PAIN

The fact that longing does not belong to the mind or the ego makes it threatening to our rational, ego-based consciousness. But to embrace longing, to welcome this pain within the heart, also confronts us with an instinctual and cultural conditioning that forbids us to welcome pain. Instinctually we avoid pain and seek pleasure, and this drive is amplified by a present cultural conditioning that denies the value of pain and seeks to alleviate even the slightest physical pain with drugs. While the advances of medicine have helped to rescue us from physical pain, there has also developed a conditioning that it is "wrong" to suffer.

Previous cultures understood the transformative nature of pain. The passage into adulthood was often marked by pain: for men, the pain of ritual circumcision; for women, menstruation and the pain of childbirth. In our society, pain has become an aspect of the shadow, to be escaped at all costs. We are increasingly conditioned to seek someone to blame for our suffering, which in the United States has become linked with material greed as an incentive to sue someone for one's suffering. To seek to blame someone else is not to honor one's own experience. To deny the value of suffering is to close the door on the transformation that can only come through pain.

Moving beyond our instinctual and cultural conditioning to avoid pain, we honor the transpersonal dimension of ourself which is beyond the dualities of pleasure and pain. We welcome the reality of love which embraces every aspect of life with the wholeness of the Self. In allowing the pain of longing we allow ourself to be taken into the innermost chamber of the heart, where we wait for the Beloved.

The mystic does not seek pain. Some people who like to live in their own darkness can become addicted to suffering, just as they can become addicted to their psychological problems. Pain like this, to which one becomes attached, is not transformative pain. The lover seeks only the Beloved, and is attached to nothing but Him. But when the heart cries for God, the lover embraces the truth of this pain. The lover knows that the cry of the heart is an open door for love, and that through our tears we prepare the place for the Beloved.

One paradox of the spiritual path is that although suffering does not take us to God, we cannot reach Him without suffering:

> By suffering none attained
> the treasure of mystic union;
> and, strange to say, without suffering,
> none beheld that treasure.[20]

Embracing the depths of our longing, we allow the most painful and deepest need of the soul into consciousness. This call of the heart attracts the Beloved, who takes us to union.

THROWN BETWEEN THE OPPOSITES

On the journey of the heart, longing draws us closer and closer to Him whom we love: "The hearts of mystics are the nests of love, and the hearts of lovers are the nests of longing, and the hearts of longing are the nests of intimacy."[21] But this progression from separation (*bu'd*) to nearness (*qurb*) is not linear, but a spiral path on which the wayfarer is constantly thrown between these opposites, turned from the pain of separation to the bliss of nearness. In the words of the *hadîth*, "The heart of the faithful is held between the two fingers of the All-compassionate, He turns it wherever He wants."

Sometimes we feel so close to Him and the heart sings with His love. Then we are thrown into separation; He becomes so distant that it is as if we never knew Him. We feel there is no God, only loneliness and desolation. Then the heart cries and cries, and through these cries is drawn back closer to Him. Because longing draws us to Him, in these states of heartache and desolation we are actually closer to Him than when we feel His nearness.

States of longing can last for days, months, or even years. At the beginning the experiences of nearness are fleeting, but slowly they become more lasting. He who had seemed inaccessible becomes a friend within the heart, a companion of love. First it is just separation that drives us to God; then gradually intimacy, the touch of His embrace, takes us deeper into love. The opposites become reconciled within the heart. The journey *back to God* becomes the journey *in God.*

In the physical world we will always be confronted by separation. Only death can lift this final veil, as al-Hallâj knew when, before his execution, he uttered, "Everything for the ecstatic is to be alone with his Only One, in Himself."[22] But longing makes us turn away from ourself and turn back to God. Longing takes us into the realm of love, into the innermost chamber of the heart where only the Beloved exists.

LOVE'S MOST HOLY MYSTERY

What stands between the lover and the Beloved is the lover's ego, as Hâfiz proclaims: "Between the lover and the Beloved there must be no veil. Thou thyself art thine own veil, Hâfiz—get out of the way!" Longing does not belong to the ego; it is the soul's pain of separation. While the soul longs for union, the very nature of the ego is separation. The ego develops as the infant separates from the mother; in adolescence we further strengthen the ego through the separation caused by rebellion. The ego's development is determined by an awareness of our separate identity. To allow the longing for union into our life is to surrender the ego.

Each pang of longing is a momentary death. In the words of a Persian poem, "The ego does not go with laughter and with caresses. It must be chased with sorrow and drowned in tears." The heart's cry for God is so potent that it breaks down the ego's patterns of defense and dissolves the ego. In the depths of longing there is no ego, no identity, just the terrible need of the soul. This need pulls us closer to Him and away from ourself.

Accepting the feelings of longing, the discontent and dissatisfaction, we turn away from the desires of the ego and align ourself with the need of the soul. Embracing the pain of our separation, we turn from duality back to unity, a unity of lover and Beloved which is death to the ego. In the ocean of love's longing, the ego is doomed. The primal cry of the soul takes the lover beyond this world and the next, straight to Him who is our deepest desire.

The lover cries for the Beloved because the Beloved longs for His lover. To quote Rûmî,

> Not a single lover would seek union
> if the Beloved were not seeking it.[23]

The light within our heart is attracted by His light and so they come to meet. This is the mystery of "light upon light," which is "the secret of the mystical journey":

> There are lights which ascend and lights which descend. The ascending lights are the lights of the heart; the descending lights are those of the Throne. [The lower-self (the ego)] is the veil between the Throne and the heart. When this veil is rent and a door to the throne opens in

the heart, like springs towards like. Light rises toward light and light comes down upon light, *and it is light upon light* (Qur'an 24:35)....

Each time the heart sighs for the Throne, the Throne sighs for the heart, so that they come to meet.... Each time a *light rises up from you, a light comes down toward you,* and each time a flame rises from you, a corresponding flame comes down toward you.... If their energies are equal, they meet half-way.... But when the substance of light has grown in you, then this becomes a Whole in relation to what is of the same nature in Heaven: then it is the substance of light in Heaven which yearns for you and is attracted by your light, and it descends toward you. This is the secret of the mystical journey.[24]

He longs for us and so we long for Him. He calls us to Him and awakens us to the call of the heart, the homesickness of the soul. Our longing rises directly to Him and meets His longing, as in the *hadîth,* "If you walk to Him a small step, He comes to you running."

We are attracted to God by God. We walk with His feet to Him. The light that rises within the heart is the same as the light that descends. His light gave birth to our light and in essence "the being of the lover and Beloved are the same."[25] The secret of love's union is that He unites with Himself within the heart of His lover. The lover who gives himself to longing participates in this mystery.

He shares the secrets of love with those who have given themselves to Him, who have surrendered the ego's desire to be separate. Love is both the longing for union and the bliss of union. Love is the sadness of separation and the knowledge that there is no separation. Only the heart can contain this paradox which is imprinted in every sigh of the soul. In the heart of His lover He cries out to Himself, He comes to meet Himself, He unites with Himself:

> It is he who suffers his absence in me
> Who through me cries out to himself.
> Love's most strange, most holy mystery—
> We are intimate beyond belief.[26]

2. SUFI PRACTICES:
THE DHIKR AND MEDITATION

*There is a polish for everything that taketh away rust;
and the polish for the heart is the invocation of Allâh.*

Hadîth

THE WORK OF THE WAYFARER

The glance of the Beloved awakens the soul's longing
for God. In the depths of the heart He calls to us and
we begin the journey Home. The moment of *tauba* is
always an act of grace, a gift from the Beloved. The
work of the wayfarer is to keep alive the flame of
longing, to feed it with aspiration and devotion until it
burns away all traces of separation. This work brings
the soul's remembrance of union into our daily life, and
takes us beyond the mind into the innermost chamber
of the heart where the Beloved is always waiting.

The heart's desire for Truth is enough to take us to
God. It is said in the *Upanishads* that if you want Truth
as badly as a drowning man wants air, you will realize
It in a split second. But who wants Truth with the same
intensity as the instinctive desire for life? The heart's desire is hidden deep within us and needs to be brought
into consciousness before we can begin to realize its
potency and power. In order to help us to focus on
the heart and activate the transformative energy of love,
spiritual practices have been developed. These practices
are a part of our spiritual heritage and are invaluable to

the wayfarer. Without them the wayfarer would remain stranded, unable to cross into the inner world of the spirit.

Because these practices can have such a powerful transformative effect, they have often been kept secret, given under the guidance of the teacher to those who are committed to the path. Some practices have been made generally available, but one should always be aware that spiritual practices are designed to create real inner changes and need an attitude of responsibility. Practices require discipline and should be followed exactly, but they should not be forced. In *hatha yoga* if you force the body into a posture you can cause yourself unnecessary damage, and this is true of most spiritual practices. Usually it is the inner attitude of the wayfarer that is most important. One should remember that all spiritual practices are a means of becoming open and aligned to the grace that is given by God.

In Sufism some practices are performed at group meetings and may use music and dance (*samâ'*), as, for example, the ecstatic whirling of Rûmî's Mevlevi Order. Other practices, such as the work of watching one's thoughts and being mindful of one's actions, are performed alone. Each Sufi path has its own practices; some are given to the whole order while others are given by the sheikh to specific individuals as needed. Two fundamental practices which are common to many Sufi paths are the *dhikr* and meditation.

THE DHIKR

The Sufi aspires to remember God in every moment, with each and every breath. This remembrance does not belong to the mind. It is not an act of mental recall, but is the remembrance of the heart, an awareness of our innermost state of union with God. In the experience of *tauba* the heart is awakened to love's eternal moment, and the practice of the *dhikr* helps the wayfarer to bring this hidden secret into consciousness.

The *dhikr* is the repetition of a sacred word or phrase. It can be the *shahâda*, *"Lâ ilâha illâ 'llâh"* (there is no god but God), but it is often one of the names or attributes of God. It is said that God has ninety-nine names, but foremost among these is Allâh. Allâh is His greatest name and contains all His divine attributes.

The significance attributed to the repetition of His name is told in the previously mentioned story of Abû Sa'îd ibn Abî'l-Khayr, whose heart was opened when he heard the phrase from the Qur'an, "Say Allâh! then leave them to amuse themselves in their folly."[1] Abû Sa'îd then retired to the niche of the chapel in his house, where for seven years he repeated "Allâh! Allâh! Allâh!" "until at last every atom of me began to cry aloud, 'Allâh! Allâh! Allâh!'" One day when he was with Sheikh Abû 'l-Fadl Hasan, the sheikh picked up a book and began to peruse it. Abû Sa'îd, being a scholar, couldn't help wondering what the book was. The sheikh perceived his thought and said:

> Abû Sa'îd! All the hundred-and-twenty-four-thousand prophets were sent to preach one word. They bade the people say "Allâh!" and devote themselves to Him. Those who heard this word with the ear alone let it go out by the other ear; but those who heard it with their souls imprinted it on their souls and repeated it until it penetrated their hearts and souls, and their whole being became this word. They were made independent of the pronunciation of the

word, they were released from the sound and the letters. Having understood the spiritual meaning of this word, they became so absorbed in it that they were no more conscious of their own non-existence.[2]

The *dhikr* can be repeated vocally or silently. In some Sufi orders the *dhikr* is chanted at group meetings, producing a dynamically powerful and intoxicating effect. To be present at a meeting of lovers who in unison profess the name of their Beloved transports one into the arena of love. For the lover, only the Beloved exists, only His name has meaning. When this is shared as a collective remembrance, the world of duality disappears, for in the words of Abû Sa'îd, "recollection is forgetting everything else besides Him."

While some Sufis profess His name vocally, others prefer silent invocation. This is the particularity of the Naqshbandi Order, whose founder, Bahâ ad-Dîn Naqshband, said, "God is silence and is most easily reached in silence." The silent *dhikr* can be inwardly repeated at all moments, and thus becomes a continual prayer of remembrance. But whether repeated vocally or silently, the *dhikr* ultimately takes us beyond words, beyond form, to the heart of hearts, where He whom we call upon is always present:

> There are different levels of remembrance and each has different ways. Some are expressed outwardly with audible voice, some felt inwardly, silently, from the center of the heart. At the beginning, one should declare in words what one remembers. Then, stage by stage, the remembrance spreads throughout one's being— descending to the heart then rising to the soul;

then still further it reaches the realm of the secrets; further to the hidden; to the most hidden of the hidden. How far the remembrance penetrates, the level it reaches, depends solely on the extent to which Allâh in His bounty has guided one.[3]

REPROGRAMMING THE MIND FOR GOD

At the core of the *dhikr* is the principle of remembrance. Through repeating His name we remember Him, not just in the mind but in the heart, until finally every cell of the body repeats the *dhikr*, repeats His name. It is said, "First you do the *dhikr* and then the *dhikr* does you." It becomes a part of our unconscious and sings in our bloodstream. This is beautifully illustrated in an old Sufi story:

> Sahl said to one of his disciples: Strive to say continuously for one day: "O Allâh! O Allâh! O Allâh!" and do the same the next day and the day after that, until he became habituated to saying those words. Then he bade him to repeat them at night also, until they became so familiar that [the disciple] uttered them even during his sleep. Then [Sahl] said, "Do not consciously repeat [the Name] any more, but let all your faculties be engrossed in remembering God!" The disciple did this, until he became absorbed in the thought of God. One day ... a piece of wood fell on his head and broke it. The drops of blood which trickled to the ground bore the legend, "Allâh! Allâh! Allâh!"[4]

The way that the name of God permeates the wayfarer is not metaphoric, but a literal happening. Working in the unconscious the *dhikr* alters our mental, psychological, and physical bodies. On the mental level this is easily apparent. Normally, in our everyday life, the mind follows its automatic thinking process, over which we often have very little control. The mind thinks us, rather than the other way around. Just catch your mind for a moment and observe its thoughts. Every thought creates a new thought, and every answer a new question. And because energy follows thought, our mental and psychological energy is scattered in many directions. Spiritual life means learning to become one-pointed, to focus all our energy in one direction, towards Him. Through repeating His name we alter the grooves of our mental conditioning, the grooves, which like those on a record, play the same tune over and over again, repeat the same patterns which bind us in our mental habits. The *dhikr* gradually replaces these old grooves with the single groove of His name. The automatic thinking process is redirected towards Him. Like a computer we are reprogrammed for God.

It is said that what you think, you become. If we think of Allâh we become one with Allâh. But the effect of the *dhikr* is both more subtle and more powerful than solely an act of mental focusing. One of the secrets of a *dhikr* (or *mantra*) is that it is a sacred word which conveys the essence of that which it names. This is "the mystery of the identity of God and His Name"[5] ("In the beginning was the Word, and the Word was with God and the Word was God"). In our everyday language there is not this identity. The word "chair" does not contain the essence of a chair. It merely signifies a chair. But the sacred language of a *dhikr* is different: the vibrations of the word resonate with that which it names, linking the two together. Thus it is able to directly connect the individual with that which it names.

In reality, He, the Great Beloved, cannot be named, because any name is a limitation. He is without form and without name, just as it is written of the Tao:

The Tao that can be told is not the eternal Tao.
The name that can be named is not the
eternal name.[6]

And yet mankind calls upon Him in many different ways, and in whatever way He is called, He will answer. Thus the Sufi says, "In the name of Him who has no name, but who appears by whatever name you call Him." If you call Him by the name of Christ, He will appear as Christ, if you call upon Him as Ram, He will appear as Ram. But the name of Allâh is loved by the Sufis because it is closest to the nothingness which is His essence.

According to an esoteric Sufi tradition, the word Allâh is composed of the article *al*, and *lâh*, one of the interpretations of which is "nothing;" thus the word Allâh means "the Nothing." Truth, or God, is experienced as the Nothingness, and this Nothingness is the Great Beloved, the "dark silence in which all lovers lose themselves."[7] One of the mysteries of the path is that this Emptiness, this Nothingness, loves you. It loves you with such intimacy and tenderness and infinite understanding. It loves you from the very inside of your heart, from the core of your own being. It is not separate from you. Sufis are lovers and the Nothingness is the Greatest Beloved in whose embrace the lover completely disappears.

Thus the name Allâh is an opening into His divine essence which allows His servants to come closer to Him. It can evoke His presence within the heart, helping us to remember Him, and in remembering Him, become united with Him, become lost in His nothingness. In the words of al-Ghazzâlî:

> Dhikr is, in its reality, the progressive power of the Named upon the heart, while the dhikr itself wears away and disappears.

PSYCHOLOGICAL TRANSFORMATION

On a psychological level the dhikr is a powerful agent of transformation. Every atom of creation unknowingly sings His name and longs to be reunited with Him. The dhikr infuses this unconscious remembrance with the light of consciousness, with the conscious desire of the lover to remember his Beloved. We consciously long to return Home, to make the journey from the ego to the Self.

The journey back Home is a journey towards psychological wholeness, which Carl Jung called "individuation." "Individuation" is fundamentally a natural developmental process immanent in every living organism. It is what makes an acorn develop into an oak, a kitten grow into a cat. But when we consciously set out upon the path of individuation this process is dynamically accelerated. We consciously cooperate with the Self's drive towards wholeness.

The Self, not the ego, is the prime agent of transformation. The ego takes us towards separation while the Self pulls us towards wholeness. Repeating His name, we align ourself with the call of the Self, the call to "return to the root of the root of your own self." The dhikr, charged with the energy of the Self, works in the unconscious, disentangling and freeing us from complexes and patterns of conditioning. One example is the visible effect the *dhikr* can have on fear or anxiety, feelings that often beset the wayfarer. Repeating His name can help to dissolve these feelings and the hold they have on us.

Within our heart we are united with the Beloved. This state of union is the wholeness of the Self, which is buried deep in the unconscious. Saying His name, we activate the memory of the heart, the memory of our pre-existing state of wholeness. This memory is a dynamic inner reality, an archetype of transformation. When we align consciousness with this archetype we allow its energy to penetrate every corner of our psyche, every atom of our being. Gradually the Self reveals its nature and even the cells of our body resonate with the joy of remembrance, as Abû Sa'îd said: "Every atom of me began to cry aloud, 'Allâh! Allâh! Allâh!'"

COMPANIONSHIP

For the lover there is a deep joy in repeating the name of her invisible Beloved who is so near and yet so far. When He is near it is wonderful to be able to thank Him for the bliss of His presence, for the sweetness of His companionship. When He is absent the *dhikr* helps us to bear the longing and the pain, for we can cry out to Him with every breath. In times of trouble His name brings reassurance and help. It gives us strength and can help to dissolve the blocks that separate us from Him. When we say His name He is with us, even if we feel alone with our burdens.

Allâh loves those who love Him. He remembers those who remember Him. Through the *dhikr* we bring into consciousness the bond we always had with Him and become aware of the deeper secrets of our real unity. The *dhikr* brings the imprint of the heart into the world of time and also leads us back to Him. Gradually we become conscious of the depth of our connection, of the eternal moment of union with Him that has always existed in our hearts.

The name reveals that which it names, and the lover begins to see that there is nothing other than God:

> God made this name (Allâh) a mirror for man,
> so that when he looks in it, he knows the true
> meaning of "God was and there was naught be-
> side Him," and in that moment it is revealed to
> him that his hearing is God's hearing, his sight is
> God's sight, his speech is God's speech, his life
> is God's life, his knowledge is God's knowledge,
> his will God's will, and his power God's power.[8]

Through repeating His name, the lover becomes identified with her Beloved who had been hidden within her own heart. The Beloved loves to hear His name on the lips and in the hearts of His servants, and in response gradually removes the veils that keep Him hidden. Then the lover finds Him not only secreted within the heart, but also in the outer world, for "whithersoever ye turn, there is the Face of God."[9]

The Beloved becomes the constant companion of the lover. This relationship of companionship belongs to the beyond and yet it is lived in this world. It is the deepest friendship and it demands the total participation of the lover. We are His servants, and He loves to be known as "the servant of His servants."

Through the *dhikr* we attune our whole being to the frequency of love. We embrace the pain of separa-tion as well as the joy of knowing Him from whom we are separated. We say the name of our Beloved because it reminds us of Him for whom we long. When we cry "Allâh" from the heart it is both our prayer and the answer to our prayer. We cry to Him because we have not forgotten Him. To always remember Him here, in this world, is to always be with Him. The heart knows this, even if the mind and ego do not. Rûmî tells the story of a devotee who was praying when Satan appeared to him and said:

> "How long wilt thou cry 'O Allâh?' Be quiet
>   for thou wilt get no answer."
> The devotee hung his head in silence. After a
>   while he had a vision of the prophet Khidr,
>   who said to him, "Ah, why hast thou ceased
>   to call on God?"
> "Because the answer, 'Here I am,' came not,"
>   he replied.
> Khidr said, "God hath ordered me to go to
>   thee and say this:
> 'Was it not I that summoned thee to My service?
> Did I not make thee busy with My name?
> Thy calling "Allâh!" was My "Here I am,"
> Thy yearning pain My messenger to thee.
> Of all those tears and cries and supplications
> I was the magnet, and I gave them wings.'"[10]

The same story was told in a woman's dream in which she was howling at the moon and felt a terrible failure and despair because there was no answer. Later she realized the deepest intimacy of love, which is that our cry is His cry to Himself. In the words of al-Hallâj:

> I call to You.... No, it is You who calls me
>   to Yourself.

How could I say, "It is You!" if you had not
said to me, "It is I?"[11]

PRIMORDIAL COVENANT

In the *dhikr* we give voice to the primal prayer of the
soul, the remembrance of God. The soul carries this
remembrance hidden within the heart. When we consciously repeat His name we reconnect with the eternal
moment of the soul in which the soul acknowledges
that He is Lord. This affirmation is the soul's primordial
covenant with God, as expressed in the passage in the
Qur'an (*Sûra* 7:171) when God addressed the "not yet
created humanity with the words, 'Am I not your Lord?'
and humanity responded, 'Yes, we witness it.'"

The soul's response, "Yes, we witness it," was the
first *dhikr* imprinted in the heart. When we say His
name we bring the soul's instinctual state of devotion
and worship into the world of time and space. We repeat
with each breath the soul's prayer of praise, the
affirmation that He is Lord. His name on the lips of His
lovers unites the two worlds, the eternal world of the
soul with the temporal world which we experience as
separation.

The *dhikr* is a practice that helps to dissolve the
illusion of separation. Through it, the loneliness of the
path becomes replaced by the feeling of His companionship. In our everyday life we repeat His name and
experience the heart's innermost connection, the soul's
primal pledge to witness Him. Witnessing Him produces a feeling of utmost fulfillment because we are
recognizing life's need to acknowledge its Creator. We
are *consciously* participating in life's greatest mystery,
the relationship of the creation to the Creator.

In saying the *dhikr* we acknowledge the heart's need to worship, the lover's need to think only of the Beloved. We step away from the ego's patterns of self-autonomy and align our whole being with the soul's devotion. While the ego scatters our attention in a myriad of directions, inwardly the heart always looks towards God. Repeating His name, we turn from the many towards the one. We turn from creation's multiplicity to the singleness of our own essence.

The secret of the *dhikr* is that the name we repeat is none other than that of our own innermost being. In the depths of the heart the lover and the Beloved are one. "I am He whom I love, He whom I love is I." We call upon our own state of union and evoke its dynamic wholeness. We bring our own divinity into consciousness. This divinity is both a state of union and a state of prayer and praise. In witnessing that He is Lord we acknowledge the connection of the heart, the truth of love's oneness.

But beneath our desire to remember Him is His grace which opens the gate of remembrance. It is only because He has given us the glimpse of oneness that we are driven to remember Him. We desire Him because He first desires us. Remembrance is a gift given to those He calls back to Himself. For this reason remembrance can never be forced. It is a discipline born of devotion and grace. If He did not awaken our love for Him, we would become bored with the constant repetition of a single word. Who would want to repeat one word each moment of every day, if this word were not charged with the beauty of a lover's remembrance? Only for a lover is the name of the Beloved always new. Love does not belong to time, but to the eternal moment of the soul. Each time we repeat His name it is for the first time. Each moment is an opportunity to say the name of our Beloved.

He gave us the grace to remember Him. Without this grace the *dhikr* would just be monotonous and without meaning. But when the currents of love flow from the heart of hearts, His name leads us away from ourself back to Him:

> When God wishes to befriend one of His servants, He opens for him the gate of His remembrance. When he experiences the sweetness of remembrance, He opens for him the gate of nearness. Then He raises him to the gatherings of His intimacy. Then He settles him upon the throne of unity. Then He lifts the veil from him and leads him into the abode of unicity and reveals for him the divine splendor and majesty. When his eyes fall upon the divine splendor and majesty, naught of himself remains. Thereupon the servant is entirely extinguished for a time. After this he comes under God's exalted protection, free from any pretensions of his self.[12]

MEDITATION

Repeating His name we bring the remembrance of the heart into consciousness and connect our everyday life with the eternal moment of the soul. Whatever our outer situation, the heart can hear the name of its Beloved and our whole being becomes attuned to love. But in our everyday life we are still confronted by the veils of illusion, by the *maya* of His beautiful world. Only when we close our outer eyes can we turn our whole attention to the Beloved. There is a story about Râbi'a, sitting in a darkened room in meditation on a beautiful spring day. Her servant called to her to come out and see what the Creator had made. From within her room Râbi'a replied, "Why not come in and see the Creator? Contemplation of the Creator so preoccupies me that I do not care to look upon His creation."[13]

In meditation we learn to still the mind and the senses so that we can directly experience the inner reality of the heart. One friend had a dream that gave her a glimpse of the sweetness beyond the mind:

> I am sitting with the group and the teacher silently speaks to me, saying, "I will show you what this meditation can offer you." The group begins to meditate and when I fall into meditation I hear the sound of the most beautiful chord of music, whose notes become louder and whose vibration fills my whole being until its essence absorbs me in an intense sweetness and bliss which I can only describe as a glimpse of Heaven. The notes cease as the meditation ends.

Such bliss is the substance of the Self which cannot be experienced on the level of the mind.[14] The mind is known as the "slayer of the Real," for it separates us from spiritual Truth which is found within the heart. While the mind understands through duality, the differentiation of subject and object, Truth is always a state of oneness: the knower and the knowledge are one, the lover and Beloved are united. Meditation is a technique to take us from the world of duality to the oneness within the heart. Muhâsibî, a ninth-century Sufi from Baghdad, stresses its importance:

> Meditation is the chief possession of the mystic,
> that whereby the sincere and the God-fearing
> make progress on the journey to God.[15]

Meditation techniques take the seeker beyond the mind in different ways. In Zen Buddhism the student may meditate upon a *koan*, which is a paradoxical statement that cannot be resolved on the level of the mind, as, for example, "How can you get a goose out of a bottle without breaking the glass or hurting the goose?" Caught in the irreconcilable problem, the mind finally gives up and the student is thrown beyond the opposites to the level of the Self, where he finds the answer, "Look, it's out!"

Different Sufi paths use different meditation techniques. One practice developed by the Naqshbandi order uses the energy of love to go beyond the mind. Love, "the essence of the divine essence," is the most powerful force in creation. Coming from the dimension of the Self, love has a faster vibration than the mind and it has the ability to overcome the mind. We taste this in the experience of "falling in love" when we find that we cannot think clearly or rationally. When we give ourself in love to the Beloved this experience is amplified many times, which is why Sufis are often referred to as "Idiots of God." In the words of 'Attâr, "When love comes, reason disappears. Reason cannot live with the folly of love; love has nothing to do with human reason."[16]

Rather than attempting to still one's thoughts by focusing on the mind, one focuses instead on the heart and the feeling of love within the heart, and thus leaves the mind behind. Thought-forms slowly die and the emotions are also stilled. The "meditation of the heart" is a practice that drowns the mind and the emotions in love's ocean. In this meditation, as Irina Tweedie describes it, we imagine three things:

1. We must suppose that we go deep within ourselves, deeper and deeper into our most hidden self. There in our innermost being, in the very core of ourselves, we will find a place where there is peace, stillness, and, above all, love.

God is Love, says the Sufi. Human beings are all love, for they are made in His image; only they have forgotten it long ago. When we love another human being, however deeply, there is a place in our heart where this beloved human being has no access. There, we are quite alone. But within us there is a longing, which is the ultimate proof that this place is reserved for Him alone.

2. After having found this place, we must imagine that we are seated there, immersed into, surrounded by the Love of God. We are in deepest peace. We are loved; we are sheltered; we are secure. All of us is there, physical body and all; nothing is outside, not even a fingertip, not even the tiniest hair. Our whole being is contained within the Love of God.

3. As we sit there, happy, serene in His Presence, thoughts will intrude into our mind— what we did the day before, what we have to do tomorrow—memories float by, images appear before the mind's eye.

We have to imagine that we are getting hold of every thought, every image and feeling, and drown them, merging them into the feeling of love.

Every feeling, especially the feeling of love, is much more dynamic than the thinking process, so if one does this practice well, with the utmost concentration, all thoughts will disappear. Nothing will remain. The mind will be empty.[17]

When we become familiar with this meditation we no longer need to use the imagination. We just fill the heart with the feeling of love and then drown any thoughts in the heart. Emptying the mind, we create an inner space where we can become aware of the presence of the Beloved. He is always here, but the mind, the emotions, and the outer world veil us from Him. He is the silent emptiness, and in order to experience Him we need to become silent. In meditation we give ourself back to Him, returning from the world of forms to the formless Truth of the heart.

Drowning the mind in the heart, we offer to Him our own consciousness, that spark of His Divine Consciousness which is His gift to humanity. So many wonders and so many evils have been enacted with His gift of consciousness. But to make the journey back to God we need to return this gift, this source of our illusion of self-autonomy. Each time we go into meditation we sacrifice our individual consciousness on the altar of love. In so doing we give space for Him to reveal Himself:

> Go you, sweep out the dwelling-room of your heart, prepare it to be the abode and home of the Beloved: when you go out He will come in. Within you, when you are free from self, He will show His Beauty.[18]

BEING ATTENTIVE TO LOVE

He reveals Himself to those who love Him, and it is always an act of grace. The work of the lover is to be waiting, always listening for His call. Meditation creates a sacred space where we can be attentive to Him, receptive to His hint. Only too easily does the clamor of the world deafen us and the noise of our own mind distract us. In order to hear the guidance that comes from within we need to attune ourself to the frequency of the heart and be sensitive to the still, small voice of the Self. We need to learn to focus our attention on the inner world and cultivate stillness. Shiblî tells a story of going to see the Sufi master, Nûrî, and seeing him sitting in meditation so motionless that not even one hair moved. He asked Nûrî, "From whom did you learn such deep meditation?" Nûrî replied, "I learned it from a cat waiting by a mouse hole. The cat was much stiller than I."

Within the silence of the heart the attention of the lover is receptive, waiting for the Beloved. Meditation is a state of receptivity which is a container of communion with God. Later the lover learns to carry this state of inner attention at all times, always keeping an inner ear attentive to the voice of the Beloved, always receptive to His hint. But in the early stages of the path it can be difficult to hear His voice when we are engaged in the activities of our outer life. We need the sacred space of meditation to withdraw into silence and keep our attention focused on the heart.

The lover is the servant of the Beloved, and it is within the heart that He makes known His needs. When the ego and mind have become subservient to love, we are able to be attentive to Him whom we love. In being attentive to the heart we are able to fulfill the deepest purpose of our being, to "be here for Him."

> There was a ruler who had a servant for whom he cared more than his other servants; none of them was more valuable or more handsome than this one. The ruler was asked about this, so

he wanted to make clear to them the superiority of this servant over the others in service. One day he was riding with his entourage. In the distance was a snow-capped mountain. The ruler looked at that snow and bowed his head. The servant galloped off on his horse. The people did not know why he galloped off. In a short time he came back with some snow, and the ruler asked him, "How did you know that I wanted snow?"

The servant replied, "Because you looked at it, and the look of the sultan comes only with firm intention."

So the ruler said, "I accord him special favor and honor, because for every person there is an occupation, and his occupation is observing my glances and watching my states of being attentively."[19]

DHYANA AND SAMADHI[20]

The regular practice of meditation prepares a place for the lover and Beloved to meet. Within the heart, the lover and Beloved are always united, but in order to realize this, the ego and mind have to be drowned in love. The ego's world of separation is dissolved in the currents of love that are activated through the meditation on the heart. Technically the act of focusing on the feeling of love within the heart activates the heart *chakra*, the psychic center which experiences and generates love. The heart *chakra* begins to spin, which generates more love, which further helps to still the mind. As the mind becomes more still, the heart spins faster, which, in turn, further stills the mind. Eventually love completely overwhelms the mind. This is the stage of *dhyana*, the complete abstraction of the senses.

The experience of *dhyana* rarely happens during the first practice of this meditation. It may take months, even a few years to reach this stage. When we initially experience *dhyana* it is usually for a split second, and the mind does not even know it was absent. Then the mind goes for longer periods, which can seem like sleep, because this is the nearest equivalent we have ever known to this mindless state. But it is not sleep, and if one is observant one sees that coming out of *dhyana* has a different quality from awaking from sleep. There can be a sense of being, or a clarity different from the "fuzziness" of sleep. Sometimes it can seem that one is gradually returning as if from a great distance. In fact, during the state of *dhyana* the individual mind is thrown into the universal mind. One is merged into the source.

Dhyana is the first stage in the meditation of the heart, and it gradually leads to *samadhi*, where a higher level of consciousness is awakened. *Dhyana* is:

> ... the first stage after transcending the thinking faculty of the mind, and from the point of view of the intellect it must be considered as an unconscious state. It is the first step beyond consciousness as we know it, which will lead eventually, by easy degrees, into the state of *samadhi*, the super-conscious state. The highest stages of *dhyana* are gradually transformed into the lower stage of *samadhi*, which is still not completely conscious. The higher state of *samadhi* represents a full awakening of one's own divinity.[21]

The states of meditation slowly change. The heart is activated and the energy of love slows down the mind.

The mind loses its power of control and individual consciousness is lost, at first for an instant and then gradually for longer periods of time. Then, in this state of unconsciousness, a higher level of consciousness begins to awaken. At first there may be a sense of being—not an ego-identity, because this "being" is not separate but contains everything within it. We begin to experience our true nature, which is a state of union: we are what we experience. Gradually we glimpse the all-encompassing oneness that underlies life. We touch the undefined emptiness that is eternal fullness. Because we are each different we will experience this Primal Reality in our own way. When we step into the void of the Self we see our own unique being reflected. With the eye of the heart we see what we were before we were.

Meditation both takes us into the void of Truth and prepares us for this experience. T.S. Eliot wisely remarked, "humankind can not bear very much reality,"[22] and the tremendous experience of the eternal nothingness that lies beyond the mind and the ego can be terrifying. We are conditioned by the basic belief that we exist as an individual, separate entity. The ego is the center of our conscious awareness. In meditation we begin to glimpse a deeper truth, that the ego is an illusion and the outer world as insubstantial as a dream. In Shakespeare's words, "We are such stuff as dreams are made of."[23]

To awaken in the emptiness of the ego's annihilation is a bliss so disturbing that when we return to ordinary consciousness we can be dazed and confused, left bewildered at the roadside of life. We do not know what we have seen. The mind cannot comprehend the Truth told by the heart. And reports of those who have travelled this path only emphasize that the mind and ego cannot grasp what is experienced. Al-Junayd describes this state with paradoxical clarity:

> Being wholly present in God, he is wholly lost to
> self. And thus he is present before God, absent
> in himself; absent and present at the same time.
> He is where he is not and he is not where he is.[24]

We have to learn to contain the dynamic experiences of the inner worlds without being overwhelmed. To realize that "there is nothing but nothingness," and at the same time to live one's day-to-day life, cope with the responsibilities and problems of the world, takes years of preparation. Meditation both opens the inner eye and creates a quality of consciousness that can contain what we experience. Slowly the veils of illusion that separate us from the dazzling darkness of the Beloved are lifted. A friend once had a dream in which she met her teacher and he had curtains falling from his hands. He said to her, "There are such mysteries here behind these curtains that it would blow away your mind if you were to glimpse them." Then he pointed out a path for her to follow that led into the distance.

Spiritual Truth is confusing to the mind: it vibrates at a higher frequency. Spiritual life is a question of speed. In the words of Saint Paul, "It is the spirit that quickens." We need to be able to contain the dynamic vibrations of the Self; otherwise we would become dangerously unbalanced. Meditation creates an inner structure of consciousness that enables us to operate at a higher frequency. Through years of disciplined meditation we attune our whole being to the higher frequencies of divine love so that this intoxicating energy can flow through us.

Faster and faster flow the currents of love, faster and faster spins the heart. If we resist this energy we could be dangerously battered. If we were not centered we would be thrown off balance. The ego cannot provide the stability and center we need. It must be surrendered so that we can stand on the rock of the Self. Surrender allows us to spin with the dance of total devotion.

But as we learn to lose our mind in the empty spaces of the beyond, we also need to be able to come back to our everyday world. The inner world with its intimacy and freedom from restraints is intoxicating, and it can make the outer world seem a cold, alien prison. We carry the consciousness that we are exiles in this world. But one must not allow states of meditation to interfere with everyday life and work. One needs to be able to focus on the outer world and function on the level of the mind *whenever necessary.*

There was a disciple who, sitting in the presence of his teacher, slowly fell into meditation. Just as he was going into a deep state his teacher suddenly asked, "How is your mother?" Coming painfully back to his senses, the disciple answered, "Thank you, Maharaj. She is very well." His head dropped back into the bliss of meditation when again his teacher asked, "How is your aunt?" Awakening again, he respectfully answered, "Very well, thank you." Once again he fell back into meditation, only to be brought back by another question from the teacher. So it continued until finally the sheikh allowed the man to meditate undisturbed. Later someone asked the sheikh why he interrupted the man's meditation. The sheikh replied, "He has to be able to come out of meditation at a moment's notice. We must not be attached even to our meditation."

Sufis are "soldiers of the two worlds." We do not spend our days in meditation but work in the world and are responsible men and women. At the beginning, half-an-hour's meditation a day is recommended. Later the wayfarer will want to meditate for longer periods. The early hours of the morning are often the best time for meditating, when the outer world is still. In the daytime we fulfill our worldly obligations, though we remain inwardly detached. It is said that the mystic must keep both feet on the ground and at the same time support the vault of the sky with his head.

LOVE HAS NO END

Spiritual techniques, if practiced with discipline and devotion, can have a powerful effect. The *dhikr* is a continual practice of remembrance that is limited only by the capacity of the seeker. Kabîr says, "The breath that does not repeat the name of God is a wasted breath." As we focus on God, He becomes our constant companion. Repeating His name we join together the inner world of the heart and the outer world of our everyday life. What had been hidden and almost forgotten becomes an everyday reality. His name which He engraved in the depths of our heart becomes the living prayer of each moment.

In the silence of meditation we withdraw from the world so that we can experience the soul's union with the Beloved. Surrendering our ego-consciousness, we gradually become acclimatized to the inner dimensions of the Self, and at the same time create a vessel that can contain this higher consciousness. At first we may be frightened of a reality beyond the mind and the ego.

But as the states of meditation change we become familiar with the inner emptiness and are no longer fearful of being where we do not exist. Ultimately *dhikr* and meditation are one and the same, dissolving the limitations of the mind and the ego and so allowing the nameless inner essence to permeate consciousness. In this dynamically unfolding emptiness the path and the seeker are forgotten. Only His formless Presence is real:

> In God there is no duality. In that Presence "I" and "we" and "you" do not exist. "I" and "you" and "we" and "He" become one....
>
> Since in the Unity there is no distinction, the Quest and the Way and the Seeker become one.[25]

For centuries, wayfarers have walked the path of love that leads them within the heart. These practices given by the Sufi masters to their disciples are designed to awaken and channel the currents of love that spin the heart and take the wayfarer where no one can even imagine.

3. POLISHING THE MIRROR OF THE HEART:
PSYCHOLOGICAL WORK ON THE PATH

I had hoped to get instructions in Yoga,
expected wonderful teachings, but what the Teacher
did was mainly to force me to face the darkness
within myself, and it almost killed me.

Irina Tweedie[1]

INDIVIDUATION AND THE SPIRITUAL PATH

The processes of inner transformation are both spiritual and psychological. The spiritual work is the awakening of a higher state of consciousness: the consciousness of the heart. The psychological work involves cleaning the psyche of all the conditioning, psychological blocks, and complexes that could inhibit our spiritual awareness. Withdrawing psychological projections and integrating the conflicting aspects of ourself, we create a foundation for spiritual life, without which any higher awareness would be distorted and could create a dangerous imbalance. Psychological work prepares the psyche for the intensity of inner experiences; it creates an empty, uncontaminated inner space for the awakening of our own divine nature. The psychological process of individuation is a *preparation* for the mystical encounter with God, as Jolande Jacobi describes:

The experience of God in the form of an encounter or "*unio mystica*" is the only possible and
authentic belief in God for modern man. The
individuation process can "prepare" a man for
such an experience.... One might say that in
the course of the individuation process a man
arrives at the entrance to the house of God.[2]

The path of individuation takes the wayfarer into
the depths of the unconscious, and involves the confrontation and acceptance of many hidden aspects of
the psyche that are found there. Through the work of
love and acceptance, the seeker integrates discordant
and rejected elements and brings them into harmony.
The energy caught up in the complexes and inner
conflicts can then be released and the true inner
potential of the individual becomes accessible.

Sufism has always had a strong psychological
dimension. Since the ninth century it has developed a
system and language of psychological transformation.
Much emphasis is given to the purification of the *nafs*,
which can be interpreted as the lower self, or ego.

The processes of inner transformation experienced
on the Sufi path are very similar to the Jungian concept
of individuation which leads the individual from the
ego to the Self. The language of Jungian psychology is
more accessible today to the Westerner than much of
the Arabic and Persian Sufi terminology; an approach
based on Jungian principles, considered within the
framework of the Sufi tradition, maps out the stages of
psychological unfolding in terms more in accord with
Western experience, and helps us to understand the
inner work that needs to be done.

WORK ON THE SHADOW

Inner work begins with confronting the "shadow," the rejected and unacknowledged parts of oneself. Through our aspiration and the practice of meditation, what had been rejected and repressed into the unconscious gradually comes to the surface, confronting the individual with his or her "dark side." Jung stresses the spiritual importance of this process, and also its distasteful nature:

> One does not become enlightened by imaging figures of light but by making the darkness conscious. The latter procedure, however, is disagreeable and therefore unpopular.[3]

Confrontation and acceptance of the shadow are the cornerstone of all inner work. The alchemists who understood the processes of inner transformation likened the shadow to "the stone which the builders refused," which once reclaimed will "become the headstone of the corner."[4] The shadow contains the secret of our true nature. It is the dark twin which we need if we are to discover our own wholeness. Those aspects of ourself which we dislike, despise, or find uncomfortable need to be loved and brought out of the darkness.

The soul is a state of wholeness. With the development of the ego the shadow is born. As our parents and society tell us what is good and bad, what is acceptable and unacceptable, "bad" qualities become repressed into the unconscious. For example, we all possess some degree of cruelty. Children, who are less conditioned than adults, exhibit cruelty more openly, as is evident in many playground situations, or in the cruelty some children can show towards insects or animals. Social education teaches us to repress cruelty. While this repression may benefit social and family life, it fragments the individual. Banished into the hidden depths of the unconscious, the cruelty becomes more powerful and destructive, operating outside our conscious control. We are most cruel when we are possessed by unconscious feelings. Then the cruelty surfaces in the heat of anger or the coldness of manipulation, and we are able to find the phrase that is most cutting and painful, or in the worst instances are swept by a nationalistic or ideological collective darkness that pulls the individual into depravity.

The spiritual path takes us into the unconscious where we must confront these shadow qualities. They are the guardians of the inner world, frightening away those who are not serious or strong enough to undertake the journey. Confrontation with the shadow means the end of our self-created ego-identity. Experiencing the hatred, bitterness, meanness, and other shadow qualities we find within us, we discover we are not the person we thought we were. It can be especially painful to realize the hollowness of the image we present to the world. We need strength and humility to accept what we find within ourself, to contain the conflict between what we think we are and what we discover we are.

The shadow is usually first experienced in projection. An individual or group that evokes dislike or even hatred probably represents qualities that we dislike about ourself. The needy individual whom we find so irritating reflects our own unacknowledged need, perhaps an unstated hunger for affection. The successful, worldly individual whom we despise embodies our own unlived desire for success. Recognizing that the qualities we dislike in another reflect our own shadow nature is the first step towards integration:

> I looked and looked and saw and saw
> That what I thought was you and you
> Is really me and me.

The shadow-projection is particularly evident when we blame others for our problems. This can be an individual shadow-projection, or a collective one like the blame for all Germany's ills which the Nazis projected onto the Jews. In its worst instances, as, for example, in Nazi Germany or in the McCarthy era in the U.S., collective shadow-projection can lead to the persecution of innocent people. When we cease to blame others, but begin to look within ourself for the cause of our difficulties, we shed light upon the shadow and are less dominated by its power.

Working on the shadow involves withdrawing the projections, recognizing them as our own despised and rejected qualities, and loving and accepting them. It does not mean that we have to live out our cruelty or meanness, but we must become familiar with these "unacceptable" feelings. When we find that an individual or situation activates unpleasant feelings in us or the desire to reject it, we need to look and think what qualities of our own character are being reflected. This initial act of self-awareness begins to detach us from the tremendous attraction of a shadow-dynamic. It is deeply fulfilling for the ego to have another to embody its own darkness. But the price we pay is that of wholeness and psychological integrity. The shadow is the gateway to the Self.

When we accept our shadow we loosen the hold of the ego and begin to move from duality to oneness. Embracing the light and the dark, we contain the opposites of creation as they appear within us. Initially an awareness of the shadow creates conflict because we can no longer live with the illusion that it is somebody else's fault, as Jung explains:

> So long as an individual can think that somebody else (his father or mother) is responsible for his difficulties, he can save some semblance of unity.... But once he realizes that he has a shadow, that the enemy is in his own heart, then the conflict begins and one becomes two.[5]

Shadow-work brings the opposites into consciousness. This is a painful but necessary stage on the path towards union. The opposites cannot be united until they are made conscious.

Initially experienced through projection, the shadow is also often encountered in dreams. The dark, menacing figure who haunts us when we sleep is our own rejected self. Like abandoned children, these aspects can sometimes only relate through aggression and anger. They have been starved of affection and the sunlight of consciousness for so long that they grow desperate. Our fear of our own shadow only increases its anguish. But as we begin to love and accept the shadow, a transformation takes place. One friend had a dream in which she was returning to her car in a parking lot when a bag-woman approached, aggressively demanding money. Looking into her purse she discovered that she only had a twenty-dollar bill. Impulsively she gave the woman the twenty dollars, and when she got into her car she found the woman sitting beside her. Her manner had altogether changed and when the dreamer arrived home the woman went into the kitchen and cooked her a delicious meal. Often the shadow provides us with the nourishment we need. It is our own discarded self returning.

THE COLLECTIVE SHADOW

Working with the shadow is long, labor-intensive work. There is no easy way or quick fix, only the daily business of withdrawing projections and owning one's own darkness. Often the shadow is not all negative, but may include unlived creativity and other positive qualities which were repressed because they were not acceptable in one's childhood or social environment. The pressures of adapting to the collective can often mean repressing one's individuality and creative potential. While some may find jealousy or anger hidden under the coverings of parental- or social-conditioning, others can recover an unexpected sensitivity or artistic talent. Most people have repressed both positive and negative qualities.

In our Western culture the instinctual self is often hidden in the shadow. It needs to be reclaimed if we are to live in harmony with both our inner nature and the outer natural world. Also, because of our culture's patriarchal abuse of the feminine, many feminine qualities have been repressed and denied which now fester in the darkness like hidden wounds. The historical hunting and burning of thousands of wise women as witches still haunts the unconscious. We need to reclaim the sanctity of the inner feminine, honor her instinctual knowing, and value her receptivity.

One result of our rational, materialistic culture is a collective denial of the mystical element. Mysticism is antithetical to a controlling, patriarchal environment, which was why the Church fathers repressed gnosticism, an early expression of Christian mysticism. The mystic seeks to have a direct inner relationship with the divine without the intercession of a priest. Great mystics like Saint John of the Cross and Saint Teresa of Avila had to battle the prejudices of the Catholic church. The Puritan fathers were also antagonistic to the ecstatic intimacies of direct revelation. These collective pressures are still active in our society, with the added shadow of a society that values material possessions above any inner experience. Many people who are born with an innate mystical sense have to confront this collective denial in order to value what is most precious. As children they may freely experience a natural closeness to God, but repress it when they find no echo in their environment. How many children deny their natural spirituality in order to adapt to a society that sees the external world of the senses as the only reality?

As we make the return journey "to the root of the root" of our self, we encounter various aspects of our shadow. We do not need to go looking for the shadow; in our day-to-day life, shadow feelings regularly come to the surface, triggered by situations, experienced through projection or in dreams. This was clearly expressed in a friend's dream in which she was told, "On this path we use the energy by putting it out into our life. We do not use the energy to go into, or penetrate, the shadow. Rather, aspects of the shadow will emerge into the light of consciousness as needed." Absorption in the shadow is as narcissistic as giving all one's attention to the ego, and it can be more dangerous, pulling one into the destructive depths of the unconscious. But on the spiritual journey the Self, "that boundless power, source of every power,"[6] energizes the psyche, which brings shadow elements to the surface where they need to be confronted and accepted.

In working with the shadow we need to get hold of these elusive and disagreeable feelings. The shadow is the master of deception and disguise, as illustrated in its ability to project itself onto others and fool us into believing that someone else is to blame for our anger or resentment. With self-awareness and honesty we need to accept our own failings and darkness. At the same time we have to learn to disentangle ourself or not get caught in another's shadow-dynamic. For just as we project our shadow onto others, so can we easily carry another's darkness or get entangled in another's unconscious dynamic.

One basic psychological rule is that you cannot transform another's shadow. Working with the unconscious requires the bright light of discrimination, the ability to determine what belongs to oneself and what does not. This is one of the most difficult tasks, because the unconscious lacks the clarity and differentiation of consciousness. The unconscious is a world without borders in which feelings, emotions, and images flow and change and easily become entangled. In personal relationships and family dynamics it can be very difficult to determine what shadow-element belongs to which person. But with the light of the Self and our own integrity to guide us we are given the tools to help us. One friend had a dream about dealing with a family shadow-dynamic in which she was given a knife and told the secret of discrimination: "What matters is where to look and how to cut."

Without shadow-work there can be no real psychological or spiritual progress. The Self is hidden in the depths of the unconscious and in order to reach it we need to accept what we find within ourself. The shadow is never fully integrated into consciousness. The ego belongs to the world of duality and it will always have an unconscious twin. But when we come to know our shadow we are no longer frightened or dominated by it. Instead we are able to use our shadow qualities if necessary. For example, there are times when one needs to be angry, as every parent and school teacher knows. When the shadow is used consciously it does not carry the same destructive power, but can have a beneficial effect, as in the apocryphal saying of Jesus, "Man, if thou knowest what thou dost, thou art blessed. If thou knowest it not, thou art cursed and a transgressor of the law."[7]

HUMILITY AND INFLATION

The shadow teaches us "the wisdom of humility." Once we have experienced our own darkness, our faults and inadequacies, we feel less inclined to judge someone else. Through our individual failings we are shown the limitations of being human, which helps to diminish the arrogance of the ego. This is of particular importance in protecting the wayfarer from the danger of inflation. Inflation occurs when the ego identifies with an archetype, or with the divinity of the Self. As we progress we begin to glimpse the infinite dimension of our own being. We have fleeting moments of divinity, and only too easily does the ego become identified with this experience. The ego thinks that it is eternal and divine and becomes unbalanced. Then the shadow brings us down to earth. How can we be so spiritual when we let a colleague irritate us or get angry over a parking-ticket?

Shadow-work grounds us, as we are continually reminded of our limitations. Yet this daily work upon the shadow makes accessible to us the real divinity of being human. Working upon the shadow, we go into the darkness of the unconscious where the light of the Self is hidden. Shadow-work begins the process of uncovering this hidden light, the king's son who "lies in the dark depths of the sea as though dead, but yet lives and calls from the deep, 'Whosoever will free me from the waters and lead me to dry land, him will I prosper with everlasting riches.'"[8] Shadow-work leads us from the limited horizons of the ego into the inner world with its limitless riches as well as its dangers. We discover the deeper dimensions of being human and are able to balance the awareness of our divinity with the consciousness of our faults. The shadow takes us into the arena of self-realization where "he who knows himself knows his Lord."[9]

ENTERING THE WORLD OF THE GODS: THE INNER PARTNER

The shadow stands at the entrance to the unconscious. Behind the shadow stand the contrasexual aspects of the psyche, what Jung termed the anima and animus. On the level of the Self we are neither masculine nor feminine and we carry this wholeness within us. But as we grow and develop our sexual identity as male or female, the opposite constellates in the unconscious. A man has an inner feminine figure, the anima; a woman an inner masculine figure, the animus. Just as we first experience the shadow through projection, so do we first experience the animus or anima, usually projected initially onto the parents and then in adolescence onto our first love. Falling in love, we taste the numinosity of this inner figure, which is both personal and archetypal. While the shadow confronts us with our own personal difficulties and rejected self, the animus and anima lead us from the personal to the archetypal world, the world of the gods. She whom we love, he whom we adore, is both human and divine, a goddess or a god. This is the irresistible attraction of lovers that is as potent as sexual desire.

The mystery of projection is that what we long for in another is hidden within ourself. Most people only experience their inner drama enacted upon an outer stage and are unaware of the power of projection. Just as most people are caught in a shadow-dynamic, so are they entrapped into seeking their inner partner in the outer world. We fall in love with our projection, our ideal man or woman, only to sadly discover that the partner of our dreams is a human being with faults and problems. With love and hard work some couples can contain the contradictions of the human being and the idealized projection. With others the disappointment leads them out of one and into another relationship, where the same drama is again enacted.

But those whose journey leads them beyond the outer world discover the deeper secret, that the real love affair is an inner mystery:

> The minute I heard my first love story
> I started looking for you, not knowing
> how blind that was.
> Lovers don't finally meet somewhere.
> They're in each other all along.[10]

The lover we seek is hidden within ourself. It is our own inner god or goddess that calls to us and entices us into the arena of love. This inner figure appears in dreams, often as an unknown man or woman. Slowly, as we become familiar with our inner partner, he or she may become identified as a particular person. But almost always the inner partner carries a sense of mystery or haunting beauty, because the archetypal world can never be fully known. The gods take on human form in order to meet us, but their real nature belongs to the beyond. They carry the qualities of the infinite, eternal dimension of the soul.

Creating a relationship with the inner masculine or feminine is an important step on the path. Withdrawing our projections, we need no longer be unconsciously caught in their grip or at the mercy of the individual who carries this essential part of our psyche. In the process of projection we give the energy and potential of an aspect of ourself to the person who carries the projection. This is evident in the animus/anima projection where our partner so often carries a part of our unlived potential. But in a shadow-projection we also give away our power. The boss whom we despise may embody our inner authority, the motorbike rider our need for unrestricted freedom. The attraction of a projection is that we can remain unconscious, and do not have to take responsibility for our own power and potential. To withdraw any projection is a process of empowerment which also carries the responsibility of consciousness. We can no longer blame another for our failures, but have to face our own limitations, live out our own possibilities.

THE INNER FEMININE

The anima and animus have different characteristics, different psychological and spiritual functions. The inner feminine carries the image of a man's soul, his forgotten inner self. Masculine consciousness develops by breaking away from the all-embracing maternal world, which is necessary for the man's ability to go out into the world. But for the inner journey he needs to be guided back through the tortuous maze of the psyche, and, like Ariadne, the anima holds the thread that can lead him to the hidden core of his being. The enigmatic feminine calls the man back within himself, as is poignantly imaged in the following simple dream:

> A woman in a slinky blue dress is singing "Walking Back to Happiness" in a bluesy, soulful way.

The anima exerts her fascination in many guises. She is both temptress and virgin, the woman of the night and the ethereal muse of the poet. She initiates a man into the mystery of his inner world, into the terrible and beautiful depths of the eternal feminine, as one friend was clearly shown when he was told in a dream, "You'll have to stay out on the streets for seven nights and every night the women of the night will come." This archetypal feminine has an understanding of the ancient magic of the earth, the potency and poison of herbs, the rhythms of fertility, the power of sexuality. In her negative aspect she is the White Witch of C. S. Lewis' "Narnia" stories who turns the animals to stone. Cold and uncaring, the White Witch personifies the devouring aspect of the feminine of which every man is afraid.

If a man is to have a creative relationship with his inner feminine he needs to acknowledge her dark side. Even though we no longer burn witches, man's unacknowledged fear of the feminine still denies him access to her natural wisdom and understanding. The feminine carries both the illusion and the wonder of creation. She is both mother nature and our inner nature, and man's collective denial of her potency and power has ravaged both the earth and his natural self. The magic of the feminine is part of the mystery of creativity. To be open to our own creative potential is to be open to the unconscious, the domain of the goddess. Man will always be frightened of being swallowed back into the mother, into the womb of unconsciousness. But if he acknowledges his fear he has the shield of consciousness, the shield with which Perseus could look at the snake-covered head of the Gorgon without being turned into stone.   .

Facing his fear of the feminine, a man is able to have a deepening relationship with his anima. She can open a man to the music of his soul and allow its meaning to manifest in his life. Meaning does not come from the outer world, but from the inner world of the archetypes, the realm of the gods. Traditionally it has always been understood that it is the gods who give purpose to our life. Our present material culture has forgotten this eternal truth. If we are cut off from our inner self, life becomes empty, whatever the outer abundance. For a man, the anima connects him to his inner being from which meaning can flow into his everyday world. She brings into his life the fruits of creativity and the joy of reconnecting to the source of life. In her highest form she is Sophia, the divine wisdom of the feminine, who brings the meaning of the Self into consciousness. Sophia connects us with the center and so allows us to see the inner purpose hidden within everything.

THE INNER MASCULINE

While the boy develops into manhood by breaking away from the maternal world, psychologically the woman never leaves the arms of the Great Mother. The girl's initiation into womanhood is her first menstrual period, which includes her in the cycle of fertility, the great round of nature. Inwardly the woman always remains connected to the source, for she brings life into the world. She feels the interrelationship of all life, the sacred wholeness of creation.

The nature of the feminine is inclusive, in contrast to masculine consciousness, which is analytic and functions through separation. The function of the inner masculine is to provide the focus that is lacking in the diffused consciousness of the feminine. Irene de Castillejo describes the animus as a "torchbearer ... holding aloft his torch to light my way.... In a woman's world of shadows and cosmic truths he provides a pool of light as a focus for her eyes."[11] Without a positive relationship with her animus a woman would be unable to differentiate the contents of the unconscious, and be unable to discriminate what unconscious dynamics belong to her and which belong to another.

The inner masculine is necessary to create psychological boundaries. Women have an instinctual sense of the relatedness of everything, while it is the masculine that draws a line and separates. The masculine provides the knife that can cut and exclude. The act of exclusion, which is an integral part of creating boundaries, is a masculine function that appears contrary to the feminine drive to embrace and include. A woman needs to find a way of creating boundaries that is not a violation of her instinctual feeling of wholeness.

The animus provides inner clarity to make boundaries and thus creates the sacred inner space that is essential for inner work. The alchemists describe this inner container as the *vas bene clausum*, the "well-sealed vessel." Without this vessel, inner work becomes easily polluted by the projections and problems of others, making impossible any real transformation. Creating an inner space, we value our own deepest needs and avoid being a doormat for our family, friends, or colleagues.

The masculine gives a woman focus, clarity, and also perseverance. He gives her the inner support to balance her outer softness, as is beautifully imaged in a dream in which the dreamer was cleaning her house when a man got up off the bed and embraced her. She describes him as "frail and yet full of strength." He reminded her of Gandhi in appearance and he spoke to her with words of tremendous reassurance:

> "From tomorrow, I will share everything with you. If you have work, I will share it. If the child cries in the night, I will deal with it, and if you need love, I will give you love."
>
> I felt as though a great burden had been lifted from my shoulders and I woke up thinking that this dream was about yesterday, today, and tomorrow.[12]

While the nature of the feminine is inner and hidden, the masculine belongs to the conscious, outer world. A positive relationship with the animus allows a woman to manifest what is within her and to function creatively in the outer world. However, the animus has a powerful shadow-side that can enable a woman to appear to function very successfully in the outer world but be cut off from her inner self. Sadly, many women have paid this price for success in our masculine culture, and have become dominated by a masculine power-drive rather than using the masculine as a way of clearly expressing feminine values. Dominated by the animus a woman may achieve outer goals, but find no lasting inner fulfillment.

When a woman is aware of the shadow aspect of her animus, she is able to work in harmony with her masculine self rather than being dominated by him. She is able to function in the outer world and remain true to her inner nature. The animus can then help a woman to integrate her day-to-day life with her spiritual life, as is imaged in the following dream:

> I go to my office, which is unusually clear and ordered. A man who is very purposeful wants to come in. I embrace him but tell him he can't come in. He goes away and another man, a figure without any external purpose in his life, comes in. When he comes in, the office walls slide open, revealing a landscape with a path. This path comes right into my office.

This dream portrays two animus figures, a purposeful man who is embraced but excluded, and a man without any "external purpose" who enters the dreamer's work-space. The purposeful man, the animus driven by masculine goals, is excluded but not rejected, as rejection only increases the power of the shadow. It is the presence of the animus figure without any external purpose which opens the wall, revealing the path coming right into her office. The man's lack of any external purpose allows him to be guided by the deeper purpose of the soul and not be corrupted by external values. He is her support, giving her the strength to live out her inner destiny.

While the anima connects a man to the inner meaning of life, the animus enables a woman to bring this meaning into her outer life. A woman always remains inwardly at the source, but the masculine is the mediator who connects her outer life to the natural center of her being. Through the cooperation and help of the animus her inner wholeness is brought into consciousness and nourishes not only herself but her environment. The fragmentation that many people experience in contemporary life is caused by our neglect of this role of the masculine in service to the feminine, which carries the quality of wholeness. In overvaluing the masculine we have become dominated by its shadow-qualities, and cut ourself off from the deep meaning and sense of wholeness that come from within.

THE CONIUNCTIO

Our inner partner is a powerful reality which most people only experience projected onto the stage of personal relationships. But on the inner journey we find that the real love affair is within us. In our dreams we taste this love, the passion of meeting, the eroticism of a lover's embrace. These intimate dreams do not reflect repressed sexuality or unlived romance. They are an inner encounter that leads towards union:

> I was in a garden party at a palace. It was a very sunny day. I met a prince.... He came to me and it was as if I knew him. He was very handsome and aristocratic, yet gentle and tender at the same time. He invited me into the palace. I followed him and he looked for a place where we could be together.... It was a very private corner. He took off his white cape and set it down on the floor and extended his hand to me to sit with him on the cape. I undressed myself and went to him completely naked. We held each other and had an intense encounter of unity and love. It was an ecstatic union, where we became one.[13]

These lovers symbolically enact the union of the masculine and feminine principles within the psyche. The alchemists, whose language and images depict the stages of transformation, described this union, or *coniunctio*, as a marriage or love affair in which the opposing natures embrace each other. The essence of psychological integration is love. Love is the child of our inner work.

Love is the "mystic flower of the soul ... the Center, the Self."[14] The union of opposites points to the Self, which is the child conceived in this lovers' meeting. All psychological work takes us to this center which is paradoxically both the parent and child of our work. It is the Self that awakens us to the quest, and it is the Self that provides the energy and the guidance we need. Finally, the Self reveals its divine nature within us. The alchemists say that in order to find the philosopher's stone one must start with a bit of the philosopher's stone. Psychologically, it is the Self which individuates itself:

> As the process deepens, one realizes more and more that insights come by grace and that the urge to development occurs not by the will of the ego·but by the urge to development from the Self.[15]

The Self is the agent of transformation, confronting us with our shadow, revealing the mystery of our inner partner, and captivating us with an inner love affair that awakens us to union. In our dreams the Self comes in many different forms: as an old man or woman who offers guidance, for example, or as an elephant full of majesty and power, as a celestial city beckoning us on the horizon, or as a mandala in which the many aspects of the psyche are balanced and in harmony.

From duality we return to our pre-existing state of unity, the wholeness of the Self in which everything is included. In the process of integration we first become aware of the opposites within us, the ego and its shadow, and then the inner partner. Our ego-identity, an illusory sense of individuality, breaks down under the impact of these opposites hidden in the unconscious. We discover that we are not what we think we are or what we have been conditioned to believe. The alchemists called this the stage of *separatio*, as we become aware of the separate aspects of ourself. This initiates conflict as opposing aspects fight for dominance or for a "place in the sun." Accepting disagreeable, confusing, and frightening aspects of ourself is a painful process. It is a journey into the darkness in which we encounter both monsters and jewels. Often the confrontation and acceptance of the monsters uncover the jewels that are hidden within them. When Beauty finally loves the Beast, the prince is revealed.

Love and acceptance take us to the stage of *con-iunctio,* where the opposites are integrated and a deeper unity is made conscious. This awareness of a hidden unity is not a single moment of self-revelation but a continuing process of integration that continues over years. Again and again the opposites constellate within us as we discover different and deeper aspects of our psyche. Integrating the conflicts of our personal shadow we find ourself encountering the collective, archetypal world where the conflicts of our race are buried. The wounded feminine, a product of our patriarchal culture, is an archetype that many are forced to confront. Her anger and pain need to be accepted and understood and so transformed; otherwise the seeker will become caught in her deep resentment. But through this work of love, real healing and transformation take place, both in the personal and archetypal worlds. Transforming ourself, we make a small but lasting contribution to the collective.

On this journey the Self guides us through the maze of the unconscious. Without its inner direction we would become lost. As we work upon ourself we come closer to this guiding center of consciousness and the light of its guidance grows stronger. What had been so hidden gradually infuses our attitude and awareness. The deeper mystery of our own being becomes accessible. Because we are each unique, this process of self-revelation will be individual. In our own way we each sense the quality of completeness, the sense of wonder, the depth of meaning, that come from the ever-increasing connection with our own divinity. The Self is infinite and the experience of unity is without boundaries. "Smaller than small, greater than great," the Self lives in the center of the heart and yet contains the whole universe.

At the end of the endless inner journey we discover that the goal is none other than our own essential nature. In 'Attâr's parable of the quest, *The Conference of the Birds*, the thirty birds that have survived the journey ask their king and goal, the Simurgh, to "reveal to them the secret of the mystery of the unity and plurality of beings." The Simurgh replies:

> The sun of my majesty is a mirror. He who sees himself therein sees his soul and his body, and sees them completely. Since you have come as thirty birds, *simurgh*, you will see thirty birds in this mirror. If forty or fifty were to come, it would be the same. *Although you are now completely changed you see yourselves as you were before.*[16]

The inner journey is a process of psychological purification in which rejected aspects of ourself are transformed through love. This is the work of "polishing the mirror of the heart," through which we come to glimpse our true nature. When this inner mirror is covered with projections and ego-conditioning, we see everything distorted, we see the confused reflections of our own light and darkness. But as we polish the mirror the distortions are removed and we begin to see with a quality of clarity and simplicity. From the seeming chaos of multiplicity we become aware of a sense of unity. The Self is born into consciousness and its quality of wholeness permeates our inner and outer life. Looking within, we see beyond the ego to what is more essential and more enduring: *"Although you are now completely changed you see yourselves as you were before."*

4. DREAMWORK

The dream is a little hidden door
in the innermost and most secret recesses of the soul.

C. G. Jung[1]

THE GUIDANCE OF THE SELF

Sufis have always valued dreams and sought to understand the guidance that they offer. On the inner journey,
dreams are of immense value, showing the path that
unfolds within us. They lead us through the maze of the
psyche and keep our inner attention on the goal of the
Self. The Self calls to us to begin the quest and guides
us along the way. The Self is continually guiding us, but
the clamor of the outer world and the ego easily drowns
its still voice. When we are asleep, the ego, the mind,
and the emotions no longer hold us in their grip and
the Self can communicate to us through the medium of
dreams.

Dreams are our own inner being communicating to
us in the ancient language of images and symbols. They
convey to our conscious mind the mystery and wonder
that are our real nature, and allow us to glimpse the
beauty and numinosity of the inner world. The golden
cities, ancient temples, and vast mountain ranges that
appear in our inner landscape help to remind us of the
deeper dimensions of our self. Dreams can speak to us
of the sanctity of the soul and the infinite inner world
whose horizons are not bound by time and space. In our
dreams we taste a substance which we have forgotten in

our ordinary life; we are both guided and nourished by the images which are filled with meaning.

When we awaken from our dreams, dreamwork can help our conscious mind to understand and value what we have experienced. Through dreamwork we can learn the language of dreams, learn how to listen to the figures that come to greet us, and so build a bridge between the inner and outer world. Dreams have always been seen as messengers from the beyond, and for the spiritual pilgrim they carry the fragrance of Home. Working with dreams, we are able to bring this fragrance, this scent of the soul, into our everyday life which is often starved of such nourishment.

PERSONAL AND ARCHETYPAL DREAMS

There are many different types of dreams and not all offer guidance. It is important for the wayfarer to be able to differentiate between dreams, to be open to their message and become familiar with their language. Many dreams are just "mind dreams" in which the mind is working over its impressions. These dreams often include images from the previous day or few days. Like a cow chewing its cud, the mind digests what has happened to us. These dreams have little or no psychological significance and usually are best forgotten.

Psychological dreams have a different quality because they are trying to communicate something to our conscious self. Unlike mind dreams, these dreams leave us with an emotional residue or quality of feeling. We need to work with these dreams in order to understand their message, for, in Jung's words, "A dream that is not understood remains a mere occurrence; understood, it becomes a living experience."[2] The first rule in dreamwork is to be receptive and listen to the dream, which is the ancient feminine art of "work without doing." We should not initially approach the dream with the masculine, analytic attitude of interpretation but allow the emotional, feeling, and symbolic quality of the dream into consciousness. We need to carry the dream within us and allow it to tell us its message. Only when the dream is inwardly contained and accepted can we begin to interpret its significance.

Almost always a dream describes an inner happening or dynamic within the dreamer. Then the figures in a person's dream image aspects of his own psyche, and a part of working with a dream is understanding what these different figures mean. For example, why did the unconscious choose to portray a childhood friend or a distant relative? The unconscious has access to a vast memory-bank of images from throughout one's whole life and also from the history of the race, and it is very specific in the images it chooses. The dreamer needs to think what the particular image means to him, what he associates with this image. Often it is the feeling associated with the dream figure that points to its symbolic meaning; a particular person, place, or other image evokes a certain feeling, and it is this aspect of oneself that the dream is imaging. For example, if a dream portrays a figure who in real life evokes a feeling of anger or resentment, it is this aspect of the shadow that is being portrayed.

Many dream images have significance only to the individual dreamer. These images arise from the personal unconscious, that part of our psyche which contains repressed or unlived psychic contents. But there are also dream images that have a more general, collective meaning. For example, one's mother, in addition to any personal associations, often represents one's unconscious conditioning, the attitudes and patterns of behavior inherited from one's parents (e.g. patterns of anxiety); while the father in a dream often signifies one's conscious conditioning, the value systems with regard to the outer world (e.g. the conditioning that pushes one towards a respectable job). Other images that can carry a general significance are: a house as one's own psyche, shoes as the way one walks in the world, or a horse as one's emotional nature. A pond, lake, swimming pool, or other contained body of water often symbolizes the personal unconscious itself. Diving into a lake could mean that one is going into the unconscious.

Deeper than the personal unconscious is the archetypal world. The archetypal world or collective unconscious is Jung's term for the universal psychic structure that exists within each individual, and is in fact the foundation of an individual's personal psychic structure. Dream images that come from the collective unconscious have a numinosity and depth of meaning quite distinct from personal imagery. Archetypal dreams often feel "more real than real life." The images and symbols from the archetypal world carry a collective meaning. The ocean, vast and limitless, is often a symbol for the collective unconscious itself. A fish can represent a part of the unconscious that can be nourishing to consciousness, as in the symbolic meaning of Christ feeding the five-thousand with the loaves and fishes. Bread is often a symbol for the nourishment of our own inner wisdom. There are many, many archetypal symbols; for example, a tree is an ancient symbol for life itself, with its roots deep underground and its branches reaching the sky, while a unicorn symbolizes the energy of spiritual transformation.

While dream books are useless for understanding the meaning of images that arise from the personal un-conscious—since those images reflect each individual's particular experiences and can't be generalized—a good book on symbols can be very helpful with archetypal images.[3] For centuries the same or similar images have come into consciousness, pointing us back to the symbolic dimension of our self, each image carrying a specific quality of meaning. But these symbols do not mean something in the way "*bon*" in French means "good." Rather they are meaningful in the way they connect us to part of our own eternal and universal nature. For example, a diamond as a symbol of the Self connects us to the brilliance, clarity, and hardness of this center of consciousness, while a pearl, which is also a symbol of the Self, carries the significance of beauty born through tears and discovered in the depths.

When working with archetypal images it is very important that the dreamer feel what the particular image means to her. The meaning of an archetypal image is in the feeling that it evokes, and Jung stresses that:

> Those who do not realize the special feeling tone of the archetype, end with nothing more than a jumble of mythological concepts, which can be strung together to show that everything means anything—or nothing at all.[4]

Combining the feeling with an understanding of the archetypal significance of an image allows the dreamer to consciously reconnect with the roots of her being, the rock of her own eternal psychic self. Dreamwork creates a bridge between our conscious, everyday life and the sacred inner world of symbols. Through working with these images we are nourished by their depth of meaning and purpose. We realize the mythological dimension of our life in which our individual destiny is a part of the cosmic destiny of mankind.

ACTIVE IMAGINATION

Another way of working with dream images is through "active imagination." Active imagination is a technique that Jung developed from the alchemical tradition, in which the individual uses the imagination as a means of consciously exploring the inner symbolic world.[5] Henry Corbin discovered a similar use of the imagination within the Sufi tradition.[6] Central to the practice of active imagination is the understanding that the images of the unconscious belong to an interior dimension as real as that of the outer world of the senses.

Active imagination can be used to consciously re-enter a dream when one is awake. It is particularly useful with dreams that appear unresolved or seem to carry a deeper meaning than one can grasp. To practice active imagination one needs to have time alone and undisturbed. Then, using the imagination, one goes back into the dream, in particular into the feeling quality of the dream. One can then ask questions of dream-figures, and *the first thought that enters one's mind is the answer.* Do not censor the immediate response of the unconscious, however unusual or irrational it may seem. The conscious mind should not be allowed to interfere.

When one becomes practiced with this technique it is possible to have long conversations with dream-figures that can illuminate problems or reveal unexpected potential. One can discover why shadow-figures have been chained up, imprisoned, or starved, or ask inner guides for help. One can also explore parts of a dream landscape, enter closed rooms, meet with strange creatures.

Sometimes it is possible to change the outcome of a dream. One friend had a dream in which a fox had been tied up by some men. My friend realized the importance of this dream when the next day the image of the fox appeared three times in the outer world. In the early morning he saw a fox cross his garden. Then on his way to work he found himself behind a van with the name "Fox's Removals." Finally, as he was painting the outside of a house he found that he was using "Fox's Paints." Jung called such meaningful coincidences "synchronicity," and said that if dream images are reflected in the outer world in this way then the dream is very important. My friend was able to go back into the dream and untie the fox, and thus help to free an imprisoned part of his own nature. But when he asked the fox if now that he had been freed he would remain cunning and sly, the fox simply answered, "A fox will be what a fox is."

Active imagination is a valuable tool for *consciously* entering the inner world and working with its imaginal inhabitants. It needs to be stressed that active imagination is no idle fantasy but a real interaction with aspects of one's inner self. It is important to have the correct attitude, and not to use active imagination for curiosity or personal gain. The literature of fairy tales is full of stories warning people not to enter the inner world for the wrong reasons. The stepdaughter who greets the gnomes or old woman with kindness and a willingness to work is rewarded with magical gifts, while the lazy daughter who seeks these figures of the unconscious for personal gain receives only a curse.[7]

WARNING AND PROPHETIC DREAMS

Psychological dreams describe the inner happenings of the psyche, helping us to understand as far as possible the processes of psychological transformation. The Self, hidden in the depths, is the originator and controlling force guiding this *opus*. Through dreamwork we can learn to consciously cooperate with the natural unfolding of our own essence. We can become familiar with the language and rhythms of the inner world, and allow this mysterious, undefined world to permeate our everyday life.

Sometimes dreams give us direct psychological guidance or warnings. This is true of a woman's dream in which there were two cages full of birds, and the birds were drinking water from a barrel and then falling down dead. The dreamer recognized the birds as symbolizing her spiritual aspirations, and had to consider why they were caged, not free to fly, and, worse still, why they were dying. Surely such birds should drink from the living waters of life and not from some stagnant barrel? The dreamer was able to take heed of the dream's warning and free her aspirations from a certain rigid, conditioned outlook on life.

Dreams that have a warning quality usually point to situations that need our immediate attention. These dreams may enact a disastrous or dangerous scene, as with the dying birds, or, for example, a car crash, which should be taken as a warning rather than as something that has already inwardly happened. The dream will thus help us to avoid the dynamic it portrays. The warning can relate to an inner imbalance, or to the danger of an outer situation, as perhaps a potentially destructive relationship or work environment.

A friend considering a business merger dreamt that he was with his prospective partner at the cleaners. The dreamer realized that this dream suggested he might be financially "taken to the cleaners" and wisely did not proceed with the partnership. Generally the images in a dream describe inner aspects of a dreamer's psyche. But occasionally dream images will reflect situations in the outer world. *In all dreamwork the dreamer instinctively knows if an interpretation is correct.* The right interpretation "clicks" as the unconscious knows that its message has been communicated.

Sometimes we will have dreams for others. Working with a dream it is best to initially think of all the figures as a part of one's psyche, and to try and understand what inner dynamic is being described. Dreamwork is a process to help us withdraw projections from the outer world and understand what is happening within us. But very occasionally no interpretation "clicks." In that case, if the person who is central to the dream is someone with whom we have a close connection, the dream may be for that person. I once had a dream about a friend who at the time had a two-year-old child. In the dream my friend was with her child who was now four or five years old, and she had another child in a stroller. My friend is a painter and in the dream she was focusing on a painting on which she was working. The dream did not evoke any personal associations for me, but rather it suggested the importance to my friend of her creativity. The dream gave her a message about the importance of painting as the expression of her inner self. Three years later she had had another child and, despite the demands of motherhood, was able to continue with her painting.

Some dreams are "past-life dreams" describing happenings from previous incarnations and as such cannot be psychologically interpreted. However, a dream that may initially appear to come from the past may describe an important event or archetypal dynamic that is still being played out within the dreamer. When a man dreams that he is being sacrificed by a priestess this could have been a real happening, but it could also be a psychological complex. Often ancient events, personal or collective, are woven into our present psychological make-up and need to be confronted on the journey towards wholeness.

The unconscious is not bound by the laws of time, and while some dreams come from the past, other dreams have a prophetic quality, pointing to future psychological, spiritual, or even physical happenings. Often when we first come to a spiritual group the unconscious responds with a dream that points out the path we will travel and the inner work that needs to be done. The spiritual journey is like a seed within the seeker, and "the end is present at the beginning." Soon after one friend came to our group he had a dream in which he was shown around a large library in which all the books were in their correct order. But on the very last shelf there were two books missing. The guide told the dreamer, "These are the last two books of love. You will replace them."

Replacing the books of love images the transformation of the heart in which love's secrets are awakened and the lover becomes merged in love, the journey that lies ahead for the dreamer. The same journey is foretold in different images in a woman's dream, dreamt soon after she met her teacher. Looking into a mirror the dreamer saw that her eyes had changed:

> They seemed like deep pools of stillness and peace filled with a kind of liquid light. They are not my eyes and yet they are my eyes. But I know that it is not me who is looking through them. A strange and beautiful feeling. It is as if He is looking through my eyes.[8]

The eye is known as the "mirror of the soul" and this dream points again to the mystery of merging in which the Beloved merges with the soul of the lover. This is the state of spiritual intimacy that awaits the wayfarer:

> My servant ceases not to draw nigh unto Me by works of devotion, until I love him, and when I love him I am the eye by which he sees and the ear by which he hears. And when he approaches a span I approach a cubit, and when he comes walking I come running.[9]

SPIRITUAL DREAMS

These last few dreams need to be understood from a spiritual rather than psychological perspective. They describe inner happenings that take us beyond the psyche into the inner chamber of the heart where the lover and Beloved meet and merge in love's oneness. Spiritual dreams have a quality quite distinct from psychological dreams. Sometimes they point out the path, or give us spiritual teachings, as in a friend's dream in which he was walking with others repeating the name of God, "Allâh, Allâh, Allâh." One man was trying to explain the workings of the world to a woman, but he was told, "There's no need to explain that. You are falling into the trap of monkey-mind. All you have to do is repeat His name."

A disembodied voice in a dream is almost always the voice of the Self, speaking with directness and authority. One friend who was involved in politics was asked in a dream, "When are you going to stop playing around and do what you came here to do?" The next day she gave up politics and seriously began her spiritual search. Dreams that carry the message of the Self speak the simplicity of truth. Either in words or actions they convey to the dreamer a space beyond the mind and the ego. Awakening from these dreams we sense this higher dimension which is never clouded by psychological or personal problems. He for whom we long leads us back to Him. Or sometimes at night He comes to us with a lover's touch in which there is never a sense of violation, as in the following dream in which a man comes up behind the dreamer and puts his hand on her belly:

> I feel him behind me, close, friendly, loving, gentle, and warm and it is as though he is "claiming" me, yet not in a possessive way—in a very reassuring way. I am thinking, he has been here, in the background, for a long time.

Within the heart the lover knows the secrets of love, but these secrets are veiled from consciousness. This inner realm is so different from our everyday world with its conflicts and difficulties. Here a single touch, a momentary kiss, carry a quality of completeness that we can never find in any human relationship. In this inner relationship there is no need for boundaries, only vulnerability. Rather than a psychological journey of self-discovery we find here the longing for annihilation, the drive to be dissolved in the Beloved "like sugar in water."

Psychology describes the journey towards individuation, the integration of the opposites, and the realization of our individual identity. The mystical journey pulls us into love's arena where death awaits us. There is not always a clear differentiation between the psychological and the spiritual. Often dreams contain both psychological and spiritual elements and need a combined approach. But some dreams can only be correctly understood within a spiritual framework. From a psychological perspective the following dream could appear to be pointing to a problem: "I was looking at myself in a mirror and saw that I was very thin, very pale, my hair in disorder." But the teacher's interpretation was quite specific: "It is a very good dream! Thin and thinner until nothing will remain."[10] The heart knows that everything has to go, every identity, every sense of purpose. In this lovers' meeting only He remains:

> Love has come and it flows like blood beneath
>   my skin, through my veins.
> It has emptied me of my self and filled me
>   with the Beloved.
> The Beloved has penetrated every cell of
>   my body.
> Of myself there remains only a name,
>   everything else is Him.[11]

Spiritual dreams prepare and intoxicate us. The heart communicates its paradoxical and bewildering nature. Those travelling the Sufi path become inwardly aligned with the symbols of love, the images that are a part of our mystical heritage.[12] To give a few examples of mystical symbolism that appear in dreams: wine is the intoxicating taste of Unity which is so addictive that even the merest sip turns us into a drunkard, a lovesick fool lost on the path of no return; honey is the sweetness of the soul melting in the heart of the Beloved; a feather is a symbol for spiritual Truth, as, in the Sufi tradition, mankind's spiritual search began when one white feather from the mythical bird, the Simurgh, fell to the ground in China. For the mystic, images of death are almost always auspicious, pointing to the death of the ego and the ecstasy of annihilation. Spiritual dreams can also have an erotic quality, as the heart's intimacies are portrayed in imagery that we can understand.

Colors as they appear in dreams have specific mystical symbolism in the Sufi tradition. Blue is the feminine color of devotion. Pink is the color of love, orange the color of renunciation. Green, the color of Khidr, symbolizes both "becoming" and the realization of God. Black, being no color, represents mystical poverty, a state in which "the mystic is so totally absorbed in God that he has no longer any existence of his own, neither inwardly nor outwardly in this world and beyond."[13]

Spiritual dreams have their own specific symbolism, but in order to intuit the significance of one's dreams it is not necessary to be versed in mystical lore. Dreams come from somewhere deeper and wiser than the conscious mind and *they know how to make their story known*. Sometimes we will be guided to a book or a person who reveals the meaning of a particular image. Sometimes we need to stay with a dream in order to realize its quality of feeling, its sense of mystery or otherness. Jung trusted the wisdom of the dream, and knew that "if we meditate on a dream sufficiently long and thoroughly, if we carry it around with us and turn it over and over, something always comes of it."[14]

EXPERIENCES AND VISIONS

As we learn to be receptive and listen to our dreams with an attentive inner ear, we create an internal space where the meaning of the dream can become known. In dreamwork, we are making a relationship with our unconscious, and the attitude we bring to this relationship determines the depth of communication. Working with our dreams, we open the channels of communication and the more we respect and listen to the unconscious, the more it can tell us about our inner self, and the better it can guide us Home. As with any foreign language, the language of dreams is best not learnt from books, but from being with our dreams and becoming familiar with their subtleties and ways of speaking. For example, the unconscious has a sense of humor and loves puns. The dream figure who "delivers the mail" could also point to giving birth to the masculine, "delivering the male!"

As our understanding of dreams develops, the unconscious can communicate in more detail. We learn to distinguish between different types of dreams and to be receptive to different levels of meaning. Working with associations, our feelings, and an awareness of symbolism, we are able to go deeper into the dream and at the same time build a lasting bridge between consciousness and the unconscious.

However, not all dreams originate in the unconscious. The wayfarer may have dreams which are, in fact, experiences on a different plane of consciousness. In the night the soul is free: "The king is not in his castle and the prisoner is not in his cell." On the level of the soul we may meet teachers, be given spiritual teachings, or perceive higher realities, and sometimes we remember these experiences in the form of a dream. These dreams can give us important teachings or a glimpse of our real nature. Since the language and imagery of dreams are usually inadequate to describe such experiences, which cannot be grasped by ordinary consciousness, often these dreams have a fragmentary, incomplete quality. But occasionally they convey an impression of a higher reality. The following dream begins with the dreamer searching for something he cannot find. Then he enters his teacher's house, and looks into her garden:

> As I look into her garden the space in which the room, the teacher, and I exist undergoes a transformation, becomes a kind of "skeletal" space, in the matrix of which another dimension is revealed.
>
> I see a city made of light, or permeated with light. Completely integrated, the city in the distance is like a great palace, unitary, unfragmented, whole. I see the city from end to end. The light of which it is composed is fascinating but difficult to describe. There are different levels or dimensions of light. "Dimensions" not in the sense of geometric relations inherent in our experience of physical space or perspective; rather it is *light within light*, so to speak. Something I cannot explain in terms of the logic of perceptions familiar to everyday waking consciousness.

This dream describes the luminous wholeness of the Self, a reality of light-upon-light that is incomprehensible for the mind.[15]

The spiritual path takes us into a reality where the mind cannot follow. In the words of the Sufi master Bhai Sahib, "Only things which cannot be explained are lasting. What can be explained with the mind is not a high state."[16] In dreams we can bring back a memory of the incomprehensible realm of light and love that is the soul's home. These memories give us encouragement, helping us to endure the trials of the path. Later, after years of disciplined meditation, we may reach the states of *samadhi*, when we have such experiences in full consciousness.

Another form of encouragement to the mystic is visions. Visions can be experienced in meditation, on the borderland of sleep when we are half-awake, or even in full consciousness. Suddenly we are aware of images, light, colors, or sounds. A vision is a momentary experience of a different dimension. Sometimes a vision can be interpreted, but in a different way from dream-interpretation. A vision does not come from the unconscious, nor does it carry the feeling-tone of a dream. A vision is not so easily interpreted through association, and its images have a different symbolic meaning from dream images. The meaning of a vision can be grasped through knowing its symbolism or through intuition. (See the Appendix for an interpretation of some images seen in visions.)

A vision can be a powerful experience. But visions are still an illusion and in their luminosity and otherworldly beauty may even become a distraction. It is important to realize that a vision is not yet Truth. In the experience of Reality there is no duality between the individual and the experience. There is no observer or observed. We are one with the experience. My teacher would always say, "As long as there is duality you are not yet there."

DREAMWORK WITHIN A GROUP

In the Sufi tradition dreams are told to the sheikh and may be shared within the group. Ultimately it is always for the dreamer to feel the substance of her dream and integrate its meaning into consciousness, but group dreamwork has a particular dynamic that can be beneficial to both the dreamer and the other members of the group. However, it needs to be stressed that not all dreams are to be shared within a group. Some dreams need to be held inwardly in silence, lest their significance or numinosity be dispersed and lost. Some dreams are too intimate to be shared even within the sacred space of a spiritual group, and need to be discussed with a close friend or the teacher. Other dreams need to wait to be told, for, like seeds, they need to germinate within the dreamer. If told too soon they can lose their numinosity or become polluted by the ideas of others. Occasionally it can happen that a dream can only be correctly interpreted by the teacher, especially if it is a dream giving spiritual guidance.

But there are many instances in which the value and meaning of a dream become more accessible when the dream is shared. Jung writes that sharing dreams with others is an ancient tradition:

> One would do well to treat every dream as though it were a totally unknown object. Look at it from all sides, take it in your hand, carry it about with you, let your imagination play round it, and talk about it with other people. Primitives tell each other impressive dreams, in a public palaver if possible, and this custom is also attested in late antiquity, for all the ancient peoples attributed great significance to dreams. Treated in this way, the dream suggests all manner of ideas and associations which lead us closer to its meaning.[17]

Sharing dreams within a group, the dreamer is offered different insights into the dream, different reflections on her inner process. What is hidden in the

unconscious can become more visible when seen from
different sides. Slowly the meaning can emerge into
consciousness, contained both by the dreamer and by
the collective appreciation of the group. In dreamwork
the attitude of the listener affirms the value of the
dream and the inner process that creates the dream:

> Through (the listener's) attitude he can affirm
> and recognize this product of the soul, thereby
> giving value and importance to the soul itself, to
> its creative, awe-inspiring function. Is this not to
> bless the soul, for what a blessing this is for the
> psyche and its dream—and for the dreamer—to
> be affirmed and recognized in this way?[18]

If a dream can be valued by a single listener, how much
more potent is the effect of a group committed to the
inner journey!

The group provides a container for both the dream
and the dreamer. It is a sacred space in which the music
and meaning of a dream can be heard more clearly.
Through meditation the inner space of the group is
cleared of many of the thought-forms and emotions
that distract us from our inner work. At the same time
meditation inwardly aligns the group with the Self and
the whole process of the journey Home. A protected
environment is created, receptive to the guidance and
symbolic function of a dream.

A friend had a dream in which he was walking
down a street full of people. Suddenly he felt the terrible pain of separation and he started crying tears of
longing. He was told that this was to be the next step.
Such a dream needs to be shared in a space where its
importance can be understood and valued. To experience the depth of the soul's longing for God in one's

everyday life evokes a state of vulnerability in which there is no protection, only the wind of the spirit howling through one's heart. The group can help the dreamer to welcome and contain this "next step."

Spiritual values are often the direct opposite of worldly values, and a spiritual dream needs to be heard in a space that is attuned to this process. For example, to dream of being executed may point to losing one's self in the arena of love. Death is always welcomed by the lover because she knows that only with the annihilation of the ego can lover and Beloved unite: "The Beloved is living, the lover is dead." The group can collectively affirm dreams that are bewildering to the mind and threatening to the ego. This provides a tremendous reassurance that helps the dreamer with any doubts that may beset her. The wayfarer is able to see more clearly and grasp more firmly the thin thread of the path as it unfolds within her.

Dreamwork happens not just at the level of mental interpretation. There is an inner dynamic as the psyche of the group responds to the dream, affirming its potency to the psyche of the dreamer and providing a container to help her integrate the dream into consciousness. In therapy or analysis this container is provided by the relationship with the therapist or analyst, which creates a sense of security that enables the client to explore contents of the unconscious. This security happens primarily at an unconscious level—the psyche of the client feels safe.[19] The same process happens within a group, except that a meditation group is charged with the added security of the invisible presence of the Self and the energy of love.

The sense of security within the group can enable the depth of a dream to be shared. Aspects of the shadow and other difficulties can be brought into the open where they are less threatening or overwhelming. In contrast to most therapy or analysis, which concentrates on the personal aspects of a dream, in a Sufi group the focus is on the archetypal and spiritual contents of a dream rather than the personal associations. The dreamer's personal associations are not ignored, but left for private inner work. Within a Sufi group the individual has to stand on her own feet and not become too dependent on others. Sufi dreamwork will instinctively point to the inner relationship of lover and Beloved that is like a golden thread hidden within our dreams. Learning to catch this thread, to uncover this inner relationship of love, is the "hidden agenda" of spiritual dreamwork.

Sometimes dreams are purposely left uninterpreted, as the person leading the group feels that any interpretation would dilute or confuse the dream's message. Learning to catch the thread of a dream, to be sensitive to its unfolding, is a work not just for the dreamer but for all those who attend the group. Through listening to the dreams of others we become familiar with the language and rhythms of dreams. We become attuned to the ways of the inner world and learn to value the stories of the soul. This is particularly important as we live in a society that only values the outer world and has long lost touch with the ways of the inner world. Working as a group we create a balance to the dominance of the rational, material focus that surrounds us. We listen to what the Western world has rejected, to the secret flowering of the soul and to the wonder of its symbols. We create a container where the wisdom, beauty, and terror of the dream can be heard with the heart's appreciation.

The spiritual path is the loneliest journey, "the flight of the alone to the Alone." But hearing the dreams of others strengthens us with the invisible presence of the path. Collectively we value this journey and support each other. Just listening to another's dream with a receptive heart allows the dream to resonate within the dreamer and the whole group. In silence or talking, we share the intimacies known only to His lovers, and create a companionship of "idiots of God," those who dare to risk everything for an invisible Beloved.

To hear a dream is to stand before an open door through which the inner world becomes accessible. Sometimes a dream will bring a sense of wonder that touches all those in a group. A magical unicorn or a golden child comes into the room and we feel its presence. This is not fantasy but the real power of the imaginal world from which we have too long excluded ourselves. In past ages, cultures have always been nourished by their dreams, and as we stand at the threshold of the beyond, through dreamwork we can welcome this other world into our lives.

Through dreams the mysteries and paradoxes of the quest are brought into consciousness. These are not just old stories told in books, but living experiences charged with numinosity. In the tales of friends and fellow wayfarers we hear the heartbeat of the soul, the wonder, pain, and challenge of the journey. We see how the path is dynamically alive, and know that we are in the presence of a living tradition.

5. THE RELATIONSHIP WITH THE TEACHER

Do not take a step
on the path of love without a guide.
I have tried it
one hundred times and failed.

Hâfiz

THE NEED FOR A TEACHER

The Sufi says that you need a teacher. Just as you need a guide to travel in an unknown land or across a desert, so do you need a guide on the journey into the inner world. A guide is someone who has made the journey and is able to point out the problems and dangers of the way. The guide gives the wayfarer the right encouragement and helps her to escape from the clutches of the ego. The inner journey is the most difficult and challenging undertaking that we can ever make. Without a guide we would be easily lost, deluded, and discouraged. In the words of Rûmî, "Without a master this journey is full of tribulations, fears, and dangers. With no escort, you would be lost on a road you would have already taken. Do not travel alone on the path."[1]

We need a teacher to guide us Home. But how are we to find the right teacher? What are his or her qualities and what is the nature of this essential relationship? One of the problems encountered by a seeker living today in the West is that in our culture there are few models for this relationship. In the Christian tradition Mary Magdalene's relationship with Christ is clearly that of disciple and teacher. When she was weeping at his empty tomb and he spoke to her, "Woman, why weepest thou? Whom seekest thou?" she mistook him for a gardener. But then he spoke her name, "Mary," and *"She turned herself, and saith unto him, 'Rabboni;' (which is to say, 'Master.')"*[2] In this meeting the love and devotion between master and disciple are evident. Mary was the first to see the risen Christ, and yet the real significance of this relationship has not been honored by the Church. The esoteric nature of the relationship with the spiritual guide, so evident in Eastern spirituality, has been lost in the West.

Eastern spiritual traditions have brought to the West the figures of the Hindu guru, the Zen roshi, the Sufi sheikh. But the seeker's relationship to the guru or sheikh is *so different from our normal patterns of relationship* that it is easily misunderstood or even abused. In particular, the impersonal intimacy of this relationship and the notion of the total obedience or surrender of the disciple to the teacher need to be understood *within their esoteric context.*

LOVE'S IMPERSONAL INTIMACY

The spiritual journey is an awakening of the heart's relationship with God. This is the most intimate relationship we can ever experience. It takes place within the innermost chamber of our being and in its moments of ecstasy embraces even the cells of the body. Yet at the same time the heart's love affair with the Beloved is the most *impersonal* relationship, because it does not belong to the level of the personality. In the West we have been conditioned to believe that the more intimate a relationship the more personal it becomes. This may appear true with human relationships, but from a spiritual perspective real intimacy is only experienced on the level of the soul. On the level of the soul we are not caught in the limitations of duality and separation, but experience a merging and melting of the heart in which there is no duality, but an increasing depth of oneness.

The work of the teacher is to reflect this divine relationship into the consciousness of the wayfarer, until the wayfarer is able to realize the true nature of the heart's devotion. Thus the relationship with the teacher is both intimate and impersonal, which can be very confusing to the Westerner. Any attempt to personalize the relationship with the guide limits its effectiveness, and yet we long to personalize what is so powerful and intimate. We need to understand that the prime function of the teacher is to be nothing, to be an empty space through which we can experience the limitless, undefined ocean of love. This was simply shown to a friend in a dream in which she came to our group and saw that all the people were sitting looking at an empty space.[3]

A true spiritual guide is someone who is surrendered to God, and is thus an empty space through which the wayfarer can reach the Beloved. In the Sufi tradition the teacher is "without a face and without a name." The personality of the teacher is unimportant; he is merely a ferryman who takes the wayfarer from the realm of duality to the shore of union. Without a teacher one would be left stranded within the ego. There are rare instances of Sufis who say that they never had a teacher, for example, Ibn 'Arabî, whose entrance to the path was an experience of spiritual ecstasy and illumination in which he said that all the knowledge which he later possessed was revealed to him.[4] But most who make this journey need to be taken by their teacher, for, in the words of Abû Sa'îd, "it is easier to drag along a mountain by a hair than emerge from the self by oneself."

FINDING A TEACHER

How do you find a teacher? The answer is that you do not find a teacher, the teacher finds you. Through our aspiration and inner work we polish the mirror of the heart until it reflects His light on the inner plane. When this light is strong enough it attracts the attention of a teacher with whom we have a connection. It may appear outwardly that we read a book or hear about a teacher, but spiritual processes always begin on the inner planes and then manifest on the physical. One friend had a dream in which she was in a green English field, in love with a white-haired woman. She awoke from the dream and the feeling of being in love remained in her waking life. It seemed crazy, to be living in New York and to be totally in love with a figure in an English field in a dream. Then one day she suddenly saw the face of this woman on the cover of a book. She flew to England where the woman lived, sat in her meditation group and cried and cried tears of love and longing. She had found her teacher, after her teacher first found her through a dream.

The teacher finds us, but how do we know it is the right teacher? The heart knows because it is in the heart that we feel the link of love that connects the teacher with the disciple. Once, as I spoke to a woman about my teacher, the woman's eyes filled with tears, unexpected and unexplained. An ancient connection within the heart had been awakened, a connection that spoke the story of the soul's journey Home. "The world is full of beautiful things until an old man with a beard came into my life and set my heart aflame with longing and made it pregnant with Love."[5] Meeting the teacher can feel like coming home, or like being recognized for the first time. As with any important moment there is a sense of destiny as we step from the ego into the arena of the soul.

But how do we know these feelings are true, and that we are not just deluded by a charismatic person or our own insecurities? In the Sufi tradition the prospective disciple is allowed to test the teacher. Abû Sa'îd was one of the first Sufis to describe the qualities to look for both in a teacher and in a disciple:

> Abû Sa'îd was asked, "Who is the spiritual guide who has attained to Truth, and who is the sincere disciple?"
>
> The sheikh replied, "The spiritual guide who has attained to Truth is he in whom at least ten characteristics are found, as proof of his authenticity:
>
> First, he must have become a goal, to be able to have a disciple.
>
> Second, he must have travelled the mystic path himself, to be able to show the way.
>
> Third, he must have become refined and educated, to be able to be an educator.
>
> Fourth, he must be generous and devoid of self importance, so that he can sacrifice wealth on behalf of the disciple.
>
> Fifth, he must have no hand in the disciple's wealth, so that he is not tempted to use it for himself.

Sixth, whenever he can give advice through a sign, he will not use direct expression.

Seventh, whenever he can educate through kindness, he will not use violence and harshness.

Eighth, whatever he orders, he has first accomplished himself.

Ninth, whatever he forbids the disciple, he has abstained from himself.

Tenth, he will not abandon for the world's sake the disciple he accepts for the sake of God.

If the spiritual guide is like this and is adorned with these character traits, the disciple is bound to be sincere and a good traveller, for what appears in the disciple, is the quality of the spiritual guide made manifest in the disciple."

As for the sincere disciple, the sheikh has said, "No less than the ten characteristics which I mention must be present in the sincere disciple, if he is to be worthy of discipleship:

First, he must be intelligent enough to understand the spiritual guide's indications.

Second, he must be obedient in order to carry out the spiritual guide's command.

Third, he must be sharp of hearing to perceive what the spiritual guide says.

Fourth, he must have an enlightened heart in order to see the spiritual guide's greatness.

Fifth, he must be truthful, so that whatever he reports, he reports truthfully.

Sixth, he must be true to his word, so that whatever he says, he keeps his promise.

Seventh, he must be generous, so that whatever he has, he is able to give away.

Eighth, he must be discreet, so that he can keep a secret.

Ninth, he must be receptive to advice, so that he will accept the guide's admonition.

Tenth, he must be chivalrous in order to sacrifice his own dear life on the mystic path.

Having these character traits, the disciple will more easily accomplish his journey and more quickly reach the goal set for him on the mystic path by the spiritual guide."[6]

Abu Saʿîd's list of characteristics of the spiritual guide and the sincere disciple gives the seeker important guidelines both in her appraisal of a teacher and in her self examination. For it is equally important to determine whether one has the right qualities to become a disciple. Inayat Khan explains that in the search for a teacher the real guide is our own sincerity:

Then there arises the question of how to find the real guru. Very often people are in doubt, they do not know whether the guru they see is a true or false guru. Frequently a person comes in contact with a false guru in a world where there is so much falsehood. But at the same time a real seeker, one who is not false to himself, will always meet with the truth, with the real, because it is his own real faith, his own sincerity in earnest seeking that will become his torch. The real teacher is within, the lover of reality is one's own sincere self, and if one is really seeking truth, sooner or later one will certainly find a true teacher. And supposing one came into contact with a false teacher, what then? Then the real One will turn the false teacher into a real teacher, because Reality is greater than falsehood.[7]

For the sincere seeker the outer world is an opportunity to come closer to what is hidden within us. If we bring an attitude of sincerity and love to our seeking, this attitude will guide us, even if we have to learn through disappointment. The Sufi says that the outer teacher will always point to the inner teacher, the Self, and that the greatest teacher is life itself. Through a false teacher we can come to know what is real and to value our own sense of discrimination and judgment.

Truth is only to be found within our own heart. Through the attitude of the disciple even a false teacher can reveal truth. The Indian saint, Anandamayi Ma, stresses the importance of the disciple's attitude:

> More important than the guru is the devotee's own attitude, because in the ultimate sense no one can give us Self realization. We have to find it. Thus it is that a sincere seeker, seeing God behind his guru, however imperfect that guru might be, will be able to go beyond the guru and reach God.[8]

It is the attitude that we bring to the teacher that opens the gates of grace. This is told in the story of a poor Indian woman who needed to visit her sick son. He lived on the other side of the river. But the river was in flood, and the ferryman would not take her across. On the rocky banks of the river a holy Brahmin was performing a fire ceremony with the ritual incantations. The poor woman approached him to ask for some divine charm to help her to cross the river. The Brahmin, not wishing to interrupt his sacred ceremony and thus have to repeat the complicated ritual, wanted to get rid of her as quickly as possible. "Just repeat 'Ram, Ram,' and you will cross the river," he told the old woman and returned to his incantations. Later, as the evening sun was setting, the Brahmin was still sitting beside the river, having finished the sacred ceremony. He was surprised to see the old woman again approaching him and was even more surprised by the look of joy and reverence on her face. She bowed before him and said, "Oh holy one, so great are your wondrous powers. Repeating 'Ram, Ram,' I walked across the river and was able to stay and comfort my son. Again repeating the sacred syllables I returned back across the river. I offer eternal thanks for your divine aid." The Brahmin looked at the old woman in astonishment and wonder. So great had been her belief in him that it had carried her across the flooded waters. He felt humbled before her and the power of her faith.

An outer teacher can only reveal the real teacher hidden within us. If you do not yet have an outer teacher, aspire and meditate so that your inner light burns brighter and brighter. It is our own light that calls down the light of the Beloved. "Each time the heart sighs for the Throne, the Throne sighs for the heart, so that they come to meet.... Each time a *light rises up from you, a light comes down towards you,* and each time a flame rises from you a corresponding flame comes down toward you.... Light rises to light and light comes down upon light, 'and it is *light upon light.*'"[9] In the mystery of God's Oneness there is only one light. It is His light that illumines us and "Allâh guides to His light whom He will."[10]

THE PROJECTION ONTO THE TEACHER

The story of the Indian woman shows the power of projection. It was the faith of the woman that carried her across the river, but she needed to project this faith onto the "spiritual powers" of the Brahmin. She could not acknowledge her own divine nature.

The teacher often carries the projection of the Higher Self of the wayfarer. Our Higher Self is something so awesome, so luminous and dynamic, that at the beginning it is very difficult to own it as a part of ourselves. Rather than acknowledging that we have this inner wisdom and guidance, it is easier to project it onto the teacher who is supposed to be full of wisdom and light. Through the projection, a previously unknown, unacknowledged part of ourselves becomes conscious, even if it appears to belong to somebody else. Projecting the Higher Self onto the teacher, the seeker is able to form a relationship with her divine light, as is often apparent in dreams in which the teacher images the Higher Self. Thus, through the relationship with the teacher, the seeker will be able to connect with and become familiar with the Self, without being overwhelmed by the true nature of her inner being.

The teacher relates not to the ego or the personality of the wayfarer, but to her desire for Truth. From the moment of meeting, the teacher inwardly recognizes the spiritual potential of the seeker and values it above all else. What is hidden from the consciousness of the seeker is apparent to the teacher, who, from his own lived experience, knows the importance of the heart's longing. The teacher will instinctively keep the wayfarer's inner attention focused on her highest aspiration, and hold this potential in trust until it is time for the wayfarer to step fully into her own light.

The projection of the Higher Self onto a teacher is an important part of the process of realizing our own inner divinity. But the inherent danger in this projection is that one gives to the teacher one's spiritual authority and power. If the teacher figure is in any way attached to being a teacher then he or she may not want to give back the projection when the disciple is ready. This is what happens in a cult when the cult leader enjoys the position of being a spiritual leader and thus severely limits the development of his disciples. A true teacher is free from any attachment and, the moment he feels that a disciple has become too dependent, cuts the pattern of attachment, often throwing the disciple out of the group for a length of time. The disciple is then forced back upon herself, and has to find her own inner guidance. In the words of Bahâ ad-Dîn Naqshband, "We are means of reaching the goal. It is necessary that seekers should cut themselves away from us and think only of the goal."[11]

On the inward path any outer relationship is a limitation. The outer teacher only points to the inner teacher, the aspect of one's own being that is one with God. At the stage when the projection of the teacher begins to be withdrawn, disciples frequently have dreams of the teacher dying. This always points to the death of the projection onto the teacher and the integration of whatever was projected. One friend, whose teacher had actually physically died a few years before, had a dream in which he saw his teacher, Babaji, sitting in a chair, dead. Then he came alive again, and the dreamer said to him, "You must be a great yogi to come back from the dead." Babaji replied, "I am not a great yogi. I am you."

REFLECTION

The teacher points us back to ourself. Empty and free from self, the teacher reflects the true nature of the seeker. In the presence of the teacher we are continually confronted with an undistorted image of ourself. Aspects both of the shadow and of the Higher Self are reflected:

> O you who stab the selfless one with the sword,
>   you are stabbing yourself with it. Beware!
> For the selfless one has passed away and is safe;
>   he dwells in safety forever.
> His form has passed away, he has
>   become a mirror:
>   naught is there but the image of
>   another's face.
> If you spit at it, you spit at your own face;
>   and if you strike the mirror, you strike
>   yourself;
> And if you see an ugly face in the mirror,
>   'tis you; and if you see Jesus and Mary,
>   'tis you.
> He is neither this nor that:
>   he is pure and free from self:
>   he puts your mirror before you.[12]

The Sufi sheikh does not teach through words, which are easily distorted or forgotten, but through a state of being. The essential emptiness, or "poverty," of the teacher creates a dynamic in which the teaching is reflected, on both the psychological and spiritual level. On the psychological level the wayfarer is confronted by her projections, while on a spiritual level the divine light within the heart of the teacher is reflected into the heart of the disciple. The thread of the path is passed from heart to heart.

The teacher continually reminds us of who we really are. His presence cuts through the curtains of illusion and self-deception. Jung was aware of the power of truth as a natural force that disturbs what is artificial in those around it:

> Because it is the truth, a force of nature that expresses itself through me ... I can imagine myself in many instances where I would become sinister to you. For instance, if life had led you to take up an artificial attitude, then you wouldn't be able to stand me, because I am a natural being. By my very presence I crystallize; I am a ferment.
>
> The unconscious of people who live in an artificial manner sense me as a danger.... They sense nature.[13]

Outwardly the teacher may appear to fit into the collective patterns of behavior, and be a law-abiding citizen. But inwardly he lives a quality of freedom that is not limited or enclosed. This is the freedom of those who have surrendered the ego to the Self and are thus no longer enchained. This freedom speaks directly to the disciple, activating the disciple's own desire for freedom. The power of reflection is that it does not pass through the censors of the mind, but is a direct communication from being to being.

On a verbal level the teacher may try to help the wayfarer consciously connect with her highest aspiration, or confront her with what needs to be worked on. In the Sufi tradition the sheikh usually speaks by hints and allusions, often saying to one person what is meant for another. This technique of indirect teaching lessens the danger of the disciple's being "spoon fed" and thus becoming too dependent on direct guidance. It also teaches one to be continually attentive. An important part of the training is to learn not to judge by appearances and to be always receptive to the divine hint.

Sometimes the sheikh will be purposefully confusing and paradoxical. Because spiritual truth can never be grasped on the level of the mind, the patterns of mental conditioning need to be broken. We need to continually expect the unexpected and not to try and contain spiritual reality within the logic of the mind. Underneath the whole exchange between the teacher and his disciples is the fact that the sheikh follows an inner law which cannot be judged by outer values. To quote the Sufi master, Bhai Sahib:

> Saints are like rivers, they flow where they are directed…. If a Hint is there, I have to do it, and if I don't, I am MADE to do it. Divine Hint is an Order. Sometimes the Saints have to do things the people will misjudge, and which from the worldly point of view could be condemned, because the world judges by appearances. One important quality required on the Path is never to judge by appearances. More often than not things look different from what they really are. There is no good or evil for the Creator. Only human society makes it so. A Saint is beyond good and evil, but Saints are people of the highest morality and will never give a bad example.[14]

KHIDR AND THE STATE OF SURRENDER

The danger of judging a spiritual teacher by appearances is told in the Qur'an in the story of Moses and Khidr (*Sûra* 18:61-83),

> At the place where the two seas meet, Moses met Khidr, one whom Allâh had given knowledge of Himself. Moses asked Khidr, "May I follow you so that you may guide me by that which you have been taught?"
>
> "You will not be able to bear with me," Khidr replied. "For how can you bear with that which is beyond your knowledge?"
>
> Moses said, "If Allâh wills, you will find me patient; I shall not disobey you in anything."
>
> Khidr said, "If you want to follow me, you must not ask any questions about anything, until I myself speak to you about it."
>
> The two set out. They embarked on a ship and immediately Khidr bored a hole in the bottom of the ship.
>
> "What a strange thing you have done!" exclaimed Moses. "Have you bored a hole in order to drown the ship's passengers?"
>
> "Did I not tell you," he replied, "that you would not bear with me?"
>
> "Pardon my forgetfulness," said Moses. "Do not be angry with me because of this."
>
> They continued on their journey until they met a young man. Moses' companion killed this young man, and Moses said: "You have killed an innocent man who has done nothing wrong. You have committed a wicked crime."

"Did I not tell you," Khidr replied, "that you would not bear with me?"

Moses said: "If I ever question you again, abandon me; for then I would have deserved it."

They journeyed on until they came to a certain city. They asked the people for some food, but these people would not receive them as guests. Finding a wall on the point of falling down, Moses' companion repaired it. Moses said to his companion, "If you had wanted, you could have asked payment for your work."

"The time has now come when we must separate," said Khidr. "But first I will explain to you the meaning of those acts which you could not bear to watch with patience.

"The ship belonged to some poor fishermen. I damaged it because if it had gone to sea it would have been captured by a king who was seizing every boat by force.

"The young man was a criminal, who would have committed many crimes that would have brought sorrow to many people, including his parents.

"As for the wall, it belonged to two orphaned boys in the city whose father was an honest man. Beneath the wall their treasure is buried. Allâh decreed in his mercy that they should dig out this treasure when they grew to manhood. What I did was not by my own will.

"That is the meaning of my acts which you could not bear to watch with patience."

While Moses represents the outer law, Khidr, who is not mentioned by name in the Qur'an, is the archetype of the Sufi guide. Traditionally, Sufis such as Ibn 'Arabî and al-Hakîm at-Tirmidhî, who did not have a physical teacher, counted Khidr as their teacher. The story of Moses and Khidr points to the need to unconditionally follow the guide, whose actions are done by the will of God. Here lies the importance of surrender, which is central to the Sufi path. Through surrendering to the will of the teacher the disciple learns to surrender to the will of God.

It is simple to say "surrender to God," but how do we know what is God's will? The ego so easily deludes us, and even when we think we are following His will we may just be caught in another pattern of desires. To learn to discriminate between the voice of the ego and the voice of the Self, the hint from God in the heart, takes years of diligence. The teacher, being a stepping stone from the ego to the Self, helps us to learn to surrender. Learning to catch and follow the hint from the teacher leads us away from the ego into the bliss of divine bondage.

On rare occasions the Sufi sheikh gives a direct instruction to a disciple. Usually the process is more subtle. The sheikh may hint at inner work that needs attention, attachments that need to be broken. Surrender is as much a state of inner attention as of action. When we give ourself to any experience, cooking an omelette or studying for an exam, we surrender to the experience. Spiritual life is learning to be in a continual state of inner attention and surrender.

The teacher is an empty space through which we can reach the Divine, a mirror reflecting our own inner light. Surrendering to the teacher we do not surrender to a person, but to the path and to the Divine within ourself. It is the job of the teacher to make sure that the disciple does not surrender to the ego or personality of the teacher. Sufis do not believe in "guru worship," which is why the teacher is traditionally "without a face and without a name." The teacher attunes us to the impersonal frequency of the Self, which is a state of lived devotion. Surrender is the natural orientation of the Self, which always looks towards God. In our very depths we remain in an attitude of prayer and praise in which we acknowledge that He is Lord. In learning to surrender we bring this innermost state of being into consciousness. The "yes" within the heart is brought into the world of time and space.

The disciple learns to surrender by being attentive to the hints and the wishes of the teacher, and also just by being in the presence of the teacher. The teacher, being surrendered to God, embodies and reflects to the disciple a state of surrender. Surrender is a highly dynamic state because it allows the divine energies to come through from the higher dimensions. The devotion of the teacher dynamically affirms and encourages the devotion hidden within the heart of the wayfarer. The surrender of the teacher becomes imprinted into the mind, psyche, and even the physical body of the receptive disciple.

Surrender is the most difficult thing while we are doing it, because we give ourself to something beyond the ego. Every atom of self-autonomy rebels at the idea. The mind protests at what may seem irrational and without purpose. The ego fights with doubts and self-created difficulties. But gradually the currents of love that flow from the heart dissolve the patterns of constriction and loosen the grip of the ego. What had evoked resistance becomes a natural way of being. We become a "yes person" to God. Once we are surrendered it is easy to follow the will of the teacher, the inner dictates of the heart. The work is then to watch the ego as it tries to trick us or draw us into conflicts with the Self. Staying surrendered to God is a work of constant vigilance.

Surrender takes us from the outer world of Moses to the inner world of Khidr, where the mystic directly follows the will of God. We learn to become an empty space for Him to enact His will. To quote Rûmî:

> Do you think I know what I'm doing?
> That for one breath or half-breath
> I belong to myself?
> As much as a pen knows what it's writing,
> or the ball can guess where it's going next.[15]

This is the state of annihilation, *fanâ*, in which the ego has lost its power of control.

On the Sufi path the journey to annihilation is made through surrendering to the teacher. At its deepest level the surrender is a state of merging in which the soul of the teacher merges with the soul of the wayfarer. Merging with the sheikh is the process of *fanâ fî'sh-sheikh*, which leads to merging with God, *fanâ fî Allâh*. This is the esoteric essence of the relationship with the teacher, which happens on the level of the soul, not on the level of the personality. Irina Tweedie describes how this process took place within her:

> The goal of every spiritual path is to lead a guided life, which is to listen to the voice of the Higher Self, which at the end of the training is the voice of the teacher. It is said in the scriptures that the soul of the disciple is united with the soul of the teacher. When my teacher, Bhai Sahib, told me that, I, in my ignorance, thought that my soul will disappear. Now how can that be? It doesn't happen that way. It is united with the teacher in the sense that it can receive the instruction or the orders of the teacher not as a duality, that is, the

teacher and me, but as direct knowledge inborn in the soul.

When my teacher died I thought that he had betrayed me. He had made me give away all my possessions, all my money had been given to the poor, and he had seemingly given me nothing, no teaching, nothing, so I thought. Then, one night in the Himalayas, I contacted him in deep meditation. He had no physical body any more, he was a center of energy, but I knew it was him. It was so dramatic, such a revelation. I was no longer alone. He was like a big daddy. I could go into meditation and ask any question, only for others, never for myself, and receive wonderful answers. What a security it was. But gradually, very gradually, without me even noticing it, a kind of transformation happened. There was no teacher and there was. There was no teacher in the sense that I couldn't see him anymore, I couldn't contact him anymore. But when I needed, only when I needed, I knew. And my mind, now used to this process of gradual absorption, knew that it is not me, not Tweedie. One minute before, I didn't know the answer. Something else within me, which is united with the teacher, knew.[16]

The process of merging which Irina Tweedie describes usually happens without the conscious awareness of the wayfarer, so that the ego cannot identify or interfere. Within the innermost chamber of the heart, the soul of the disciple is united with the soul of the teacher. Through this initial state of union the disciple is led to a state of union with God. On the level of the ego we will always remain separate. But within the heart we come to know the secret of love's union, as Rûmî describes, speaking of his beloved Shams: "O seeker! Why do I say me or him, when he is myself and I am he? Yes, all is him and I am contained in him."[17]

THE TEACHER AND THE GROUP

The teacher is the representative of a spiritual lineage or tradition, each of which has its own practices and qualities.[18] But in essence a spiritual tradition is a ray of energy which transforms the seeker and takes her Home. The work of the teacher is to be the "caretaker" of this energy, which is passed from teacher to disciple in an uninterrupted chain of succession. If the teacher remains aligned to the inner tradition of his lineage, this energy is available for those who are attracted to the path.

To make a connection with a teacher is to make a connection with the energy of the path. This is what attracts a seeker to a particular teacher or path. The different Sufi orders have different qualities of energy which are suited to different individuals. Souls are different and need different forms of spiritual nourishment. Even within a particular group each seeker will be treated individually, for it is the job of the teacher to give the seeker what he or she needs. This was simply imaged in a dream in which the teacher is a shopkeeper standing behind the counter providing for the needs of those who come.

In this dream the dreamer is very aware that although the teacher doesn't ask for money, things are not free. On the spiritual path money is never charged for teaching; as a friend was told when he first met his teacher, "Here no money is charged. You pay with yourself."

Not all those attracted to a Sufi teacher will remain on the path. Only a few are prepared to pay the price for the whole Truth, for "who wants to get rid of the ego?" Some people come for a little bit of Truth. They are not prepared to give up everything. One woman who wrote poetry came to my teacher and said that she wanted the whole Truth. The teacher asked her about the poetry and she said that she couldn't give that up. It came to her through an inner guide and people enjoyed it. So the teacher said, "Why not be satisfied with that?" For the whole Truth one must give up everything, which does not mean giving everything away, but being unattached. Real poverty, says the Sufi, is the poverty of the heart.

The teacher never judges, but respects the spiritual destiny of the seeker. People come for what they need. It may be that an individual just needs a certain nourishment at a certain stage in his or her spiritual development. And although it is said that "there is only one teacher, only one spiritual guide in the whole world, for each of us,"[19] it is also a part of the Sufi tradition that wayfarers may need to spend time with different teachers, sometimes being specifically sent by one sheikh to another sheikh.

The energy of the path is always present at group meetings. Coming to the group is like "charging up the batteries," giving the wayfarer the energy necessary to keep the inner attention focused on the goal despite all the distractions of the outer world. Group meetings are an important part of the Sufi tradition, and are usually held once or twice a week. Meditation, *dhikr*, *samâ'* (music and dance), dreamwork, and discussion (whatever activities belong to a particular Sufi order) are performed within the group. The thirteenth-century Sufi, Bahâ ad-Dîn Naqshband, said, "Ours is the way of group discussion. In solitude there is renown and in renown there is danger." A story about a pupil of al-Junayd points to the same danger:

A disciple formed the notion that he had attained a degree of perfection.

"It is better for me to be alone," he thought.

So he withdrew into a corner and sat there for a space. Every night he had the experience of being brought a camel, and was told "We will take you to Paradise." He would sit on the camel until he arrived at a pleasant and cheerful spot thronged with handsome folk and abounding in choice dishes and running water. There he would remain until dawn; then he would fall asleep and awake to find himself in his cell. He now became very proud and conceited.

"Every night I am taken to Paradise," he would boast.

His words came to Junayd's ears. He at once arose and proceeded to his cell, where he found him putting on the greatest airs. Junayd asked him what had happened and he told the whole story to the sheikh.

"Tonight when you are taken there," Junayd told him, "say thrice, 'There is no strength nor power save with God, the Sublime, the Almighty.'"

That night the disciple was transported as usual. He disbelieved in his heart what the sheikh had told him; nevertheless, when he reached that place he uttered as an experiment, "There is no strength nor power." The company all screamed and fled, and he found himself sitting on a dunghill with bones lying before him. Realizing his error, he repented and repaired to Junayd's circle. He

had learned that for a disciple to dwell alone is
mortal poison.[20]

This story shows both the danger of seclusion and the
need for the sheikh to help the wayfarer distinguish
between true and false visions. Becoming inflated, one
can easily lose the path.

The group provides both psychological friction
(the shadow is more easily visible in the presence of
others) and spiritual company. Spiritual values are so
different from those of the world it is easy for a seeker
to feel isolated or doubt the value of the quest. There is
a special companionship of those who "love one another for God's sake." Fellow travellers inspire each other
with the desire for truth. The more committed help the
others to catch the thread of their own devotion and
to persevere despite all the difficulties:

> You may be happy enough going along,
> but with others you'll get farther, and faster.
>
> Someone who goes cheerfully by himself
> to the customs house to pay his traveller's tax
> will go even more lightheartedly
> when friends are with him.
>
> Every prophet sought out companions.
> A wall standing alone is useless,
> but put three or four walls together,
> and they'll support a roof and keep
> the grain dry and safe.[21]

The teacher is the focus for the group, keeping the
group inwardly aligned with the energy of the path. In
Sufi symbolism the sheikh is the "pole" (*qutb*), a central

connection to the higher dimensions. Like the pole of a tent, the sheikh supports an enclosed, protected space within which wayfarers are able to come closer to something within themselves. But because the essence of the link between the sheikh and the wayfarer is on the inner plane of the soul, *a group can function without the physical presence of the sheikh.* If one or two members of the group are inwardly committed to the path they will connect the group with the energy of the teacher and the tradition. This group will be magnetically aligned to the path, and will be protected and nourished by the energy of the chain of transmission.

A spiritual group of committed seekers is a dynamic spiritual center. The group provides a container for inner work and a sacred space for meditation. Meditating with others increases the energy of love, making the meditation stronger. If three people are meditating together they are five or six times as powerful as when one person meditates. And if their hearts are crying with longing and the desire for Truth, they are a hundred times as powerful. When our hearts are turned towards God we channel the energy of remembrance and make conscious the link of love between the Creator and his creation. This energy helps all those who come to the group, and it also creates a point of light on the inner planes.

When an individual goes into meditation, the energy of love spins the heart. A group of sincere seekers also spins with the energy of love. The group is contained by love and also contains this divine power. The group becomes a transformative space that helps to attune the world to love. Sufis are servants of humanity, and in the silence of their devotion they infuse the world with the remembrance of God.

THE DIVINE SUBSTANCE WITHIN THE HEART

The group is held within the heart of the teacher, who is held within the heart of his teacher, even if he is no longer physically alive. The energy of the path is a containment in love. All those who have walked the path before us guide us with their invisible footprints. Without the teacher or the group we would be left stranded in a world of illusion. Yet at the same time the soul's journey is a solitary undertaking: "Solitary, God loves only the solitary—One, He loves only him who witnesses Him as One."[22] Only in our aloneness can we come closer to Him who is One and Alone.

The work of the teacher is to keep the wayfarer's attention always on the goal and the fire of devotion burning. The fire of devotion within the heart, ignited by the glance of the Beloved, contains the secret of divine consciousness, *sirr Allâh*. *Sirr Allâh* is a spiritual substance within the innermost chamber of the heart, the heart of hearts. His divine consciousness, which reveals itself within the heart of His devoted servant, is at once the wayfarer, the path, and the real teacher:

> I am transcendent reality, and I am the tenuous thread that brings it very close. I am the secret of man in his very act of existing, and I am the invisible one who is the object of worship.... I am the sheikh with the divine nature, and I am the guardian of the world of human nature.[23]

From the moment we meet our teacher, a link is made that connects us back to this essence within the heart. What we look for in the sheikh is this divine consciousness that contains the deepest purpose of our incarnation. The sheikh, attuned to the frequency of the soul, recognizes and reflects back this hidden secret. He is the mediator between the wayfarer and the wayfarer's own divine nature, always aware that "the only guide to God is God Himself."[24]

Surrendering to the teacher, the wayfarer is thrown into the arena of her own heart where the real process of transformation takes place. The heart is remade so that it is able to contain the higher frequencies of love without being overwhelmed or fragmented. The teacher is the guardian of this process, the caretaker of the energy of transformation. The path prepares and opens us to an awareness of "what we were before we were," the primordial oneness of the Self. On the level of the soul the teacher and wayfarer merge together as the wayfarer experiences what was always, in fact, the true nature of this relationship. The light within the teacher calls to the light within the wayfarer but it is really one light, calling to itself, evoking itself, merging with itself. Within the heart it is *light upon light.*

6. UNITING THE TWO WORLDS

The true mystic goes in and out amongst the people
and eats and sleeps with them
and buys and sells in the market and marries
and takes part in social intercourse,
and never forgets God for a single moment.

Abû Sa'îd ibn Abî 'l-Khayr[1]

IN THE WORLD BUT NOT OF THE WORLD

Sufism is not an ascetic or monastic path. The wayfarer aspires to realize God while living an everyday life, having a family, a job, or other worldly responsibilities. Learning to live an outer life in the world and at the same time keep the inner attention focused on the Beloved is a cornerstone of the Sufi path, characterized in the saying "in the world but not of the world."

Sufis are known as "slaves of the One and servants of the many." Belonging to God, they work in the world, bringing light and love into the marketplace of ordinary life. If they were recluses living in the desert or mountain caves they could not perform this work. Many Sufi masters have been craftsmen, carpenters, potters, or shoemakers, teaching both disciples and apprentices. Integrating the inner and outer life, Sufis enable the light of the beyond to flow into everyday life, serving the Creator in the midst of His creation.

In order to be of service to the Creator, the lover needs to become free of the ego's attachments to the world; otherwise we merely serve the ego and not the will of God. Every mystical path is a process of freeing the seeker from the grip of desires and the web of the illusion of this world. Some paths achieve this through seclusion, retiring from the world into a monastery or hermitage; through taking a vow of poverty, wearing the orange robe of a *sannyasin*; or through some other forms of detachment. For the Sufi, real poverty is the poverty of the heart, an inner state of non-attachment. To quote Hujwîrî, "The poor man is not he whose hand is empty of provisions but he whose nature is empty of desires."[2] The Sufi seeks to realize this state of poverty while living in the midst of the world with all of its myriad attractions.

Seeking inner freedom, we are confronted by the question: how can the ego renounce the ego? Any attempt to renounce our attachments evokes the danger of repression: the ego just represses an attachment which then grips us from within. This is illustrated in 'Attâr's story of the dervish who was attached to his long flowing beard:

> In the time of Moses there was a dervish who rigorously performed his spiritual exercises and prayers, but had not achieved any inner realization or spiritual experiences. He had a long, beautiful beard, and often while praying, would stop to comb it. One day, seeing Moses, the dervish went to him and said, "Please ask God to tell me why I experience neither spiritual satisfaction nor ecstasy."
>
> The next time Moses went up on Mount Sinai he spoke to God about the dervish, and God said, in a tone of displeasure, "Although this dervish has sought union with Me, nevertheless

he is constantly thinking about his beard." When Moses told the dervish what God had said, the dervish wept and immediately began tearing out his magnificent beard.

A year passed and Moses was on his way to Mount Sinai when he met the beardless dervish. Once again the dervish complained that despite all his practices and efforts he had no experiences. When Moses was with God he again asked about the dervish. He received the reply, "He is still thinking about his beard!"[3]

The dervish, free of his physical beard, was still inwardly attached to his beard. The obstacle remained, and because it was invisible it was even more difficult to remove.

Furthermore, just as we can be attached to the world, so can we become attached to the idea of renunciation. To outwardly renounce the world can just give the ego another identity, which, because it is "spiritual," may be even more of a problem to eradicate. The ego can glorify in its state of renunciation, making all our efforts useless. In the ninth century the Sufis of Nîshâpûr realized the danger of the ego's identifying with the spiritual quest: this spiritual identity only strengthens the ego. Many Sufis of the time could be recognized by the special patch-frock garments they wore, and so the Nîshâpûr Sufis wore only ordinary clothes. This attitude became integrated into the Naqsh-bandi Sufi tradition, which stressed the idea of "solitude in the crowd—outwardly to be with the people, inwardly to be with God." Living an ordinary life within the community, dressing like everyone else, the wayfarer is less likely to be caught by spiritual attachments. She is also able to be more integrated within the community, working with people without the barrier that a spiritual or religious appearance might evoke.

The Sufi does not primarily seek to be free of this world but to be reunited with the Beloved. In order to return to God and be of service to Him we need to become detached, but this detachment is achieved not through renunciation of the world but rather through our attitude of devotion to Him. Spiritual poverty is to be inwardly dependent upon God. He frees us from the chains of His world. Because we love Him He lifts the veils of illusion, the *maya* of this world, that separate us from Him. Remembering Him we forget all else, as He turns the heart of His lover away from the world back to Him. In the midst of the marketplace we look only towards God, and He reveals the secret of His Oneness, that there is nothing other than He:

> The existence of the beggar is His existence and the existence of the sick is His existence. Now when this is admitted, it is acknowledged that this existence is His existence and that the existence of all created things is His existence, and when the secret of one atom of the atom is clear, the secret of all created things, both outward and inward, is clear, and you do not see in this world or the next, anything except God.[4]

THERE IS NO GOD BUT GOD

In the moment of *tauba* He reveals the secret of His Oneness within the heart of His lover. For a moment the heart tastes the Truth of unity, only to be thrown into the pain of separation. Then begins the long and painful process of turning away from the world and turning back to God. The exile begins to retrace her footsteps back to the Source, and confronts the pain of exile. Remembering that we belong Somewhere, we are forced to recognize that we are a stranger in this world, a traveller passing through. For some this evokes a joyful feeling of confirmation, as a sense of alienation that we have always carried finally makes sense. We know why we have felt an outcast, not fitting into the world around us. For others, this recognition of our alien condition evokes a fear of the unknown, and of the drunken desire of the soul which would gamble away everything for one taste of the Beloved. When one friend came to our group she had a dream in which she was being taken to a gambling casino full of drunkards, and while she was there her car was totally wrecked! Only idiots would gamble everything the world values for an invisible Beloved. Yet this is what the soul longs for. Bahâ ad-Dîn Naqshband said that he learned utter devotion to the search for Truth from a gambler:

> I watched a gambler lose everything he possessed and when a comrade begged him to give it up, he answered: "Ah, my friend, if I had to give my head for this game, I could not do without it." When I heard this, my heart was flooded with amazement and ever since I have pursued Truth with the same single-mindedness.[5]

The process of turning away from the world and turning back to God is encapsulated in the *shahâda*, the saying *"lâ ilâha illâ 'llâh"* ("There is no god but God"). The *shahâda* is composed of two elements: the negation, *lâ ilâha* ("there is no god"); and the affirmation, *illâ 'llâh* ("but God"). The negation is the sword that cuts us away from the world of illusion, turning our attention inward. Every spiritual path teaches that Truth is to be found within us. In the words of Saint Luke, "The kingdom of God is within you."[6] The purpose of the negation is the affirmation of Allâh. We negate the world in order to affirm that He Alone is God.

The affirmation of Allâh is mankind's primordial covenant with God. When He asked the not-yet-created humanity, "Am I not your Lord?" they answered, "Yes, we witness it." This "yes" is the soul's affirmation hidden within the heart. Recognizing the illusion of the world, we affirm that it is totally dependent upon Him who gives it substance and meaning. We affirm that He is Lord. The spiritual path takes us away from the fascinating multiplicity of creation to a realization of the underlying oneness it reflects. We learn that:

> ... in everything there is a witness for Him
> that points to the fact that He is One.[7]

THE DARK NIGHT OF THE SOUL

The journey from multiplicity towards union begins with the painful awareness that we are separate from God, that we live as exiles in a world without meaning. What we glimpse within the heart is hidden from us in the world, and so we instinctively turn inward towards this taste of Truth. We do not renounce the world. It gradually falls away as something infinitely more precious is revealed. If you have ten dollars in one pocket and that is all you possess, it is of great importance. But if someone puts ten-thousand dollars in your other pocket, the ten dollars lose their importance. This is what happens inwardly as a doorway to the beyond is opened within the heart. We sense that there is something that can fulfill us more than all the attractions in the world can.

In the West we have become so conditioned by an ego-oriented psychology in which everything depends upon the effort and will of the individual that we easily forget the primal spiritual truth: *we are taken by God to God.* We begin the quest because He desires us. Seducing us with the secrets of love, He turns our attention inward:

> in the end
> a man tires of everything
> except heart's desiring,
> soul's journeying
>
> sultan, saint, pickpocket;
> love has everyone by the ear
> dragging us to God
> by secret ways
>
> I never knew
> that God, too, desires us[8]

A glimpse of His beauty, a taste of His love, turns our attention away from the outer world, which slowly loses its attraction. Our focus has been redirected and friends and activities that used to interest us no longer hold our attention. Then the doors of the world close behind us and we are awakened to a sense of desolation as we find that nothing we know fulfills us. In this desert we are left to wander alone. It is a landscape every wayfarer must pass through, what Saint John of the Cross called "the Dark Night of the Soul." One friend described how she had two months of bliss followed by two years of despair. This period of transition is a most difficult time in which we feel forsaken and destitute. The outer world and our everyday life can appear meaningless and yet the door to the inner world seems closed. We are left with our longing.

But in this desert we are being tested and prepared. Can we bear the loneliness of the journey? Do we have the perseverance to stick to our desire for Truth? Perseverance is one of the most important qualities for the wayfarer, who is continually confronted by difficult or seemingly impossible situations. We must continue in spite of everything, even when the teacher puts all appearances against him and may appear to let us down or betray us. The ego is terrified by the dimension of the Self and fights with all its powers. We are bombarded with doubts and sensible reasons for avoiding the journey or avoiding ourself. The world may suddenly present us with exciting diversions or seemingly worthwhile causes, which, when we look closely, are just ego-attractions. It is then that we need the sword of *lâ ilâha* to cut away these illusions and *illâ 'llâh,* the affirmation of the heart's deepest dream, to keep us focused on the goal.

Whatever the difficulties, each day is an opportunity to come closer to Him whom we love, each moment a chance to repeat His name. There is a pride that pushes us onward, a pride that says, "Others have made this journey before me and I am not less than they." There are two forms of pride, the pride of the ego and the pride of the Self. The pride of the ego, the arrogance that says, "I am better than you," is an obstacle and needs to be replaced with humility. But the pride of the Self is the deep dignity of the human being that demands the best of us. The pride of the Self will push us beyond our known limits and make us persevere, whatever confronts us.

During this time in the desert the values that attached us to the ego and the world are gradually dissolved. Life may appear to lack purpose, but it is because we are creating a space for a deeper purpose to manifest. A student once came to a Zen master for spiritual teachings. The master poured him a cup of tea. To the student's dismay the teacher continued pouring the tea even when the cup was full and overflowing. Eventually the student could no longer restrain himself, and exclaimed to the master that the cup was full and overflowing. The master replied, "And you come to me with your cup already full and expect teaching!" First the cup has to be emptied before it can be filled with the substance of the path.

During this period of detachment from the world, it is important that we do not seek a new mode of outer fulfillment. Because we are conditioned to believe that meaning comes from our outer circumstances, we may look for a new job or a new relationship to fill the emptiness and lack of meaning. To do so would be counterproductive. We have to learn the feminine wisdom of patience and "work without doing." Holding the space of unfulfillment and not allowing the ego to fill it with a new pattern of attachment is the work that needs to be done. I once had a dream that pointed to this dynamic:

> I am with my teacher's teacher, Bhai Sahib, who asks me to get him a chocolate Easter egg. I search the nearby town but cannot find an Easter egg. When I return to where Bhai Sahib had been he has gone. I am told that he could not wait for me.

I awoke from this dream in despair. The one time that Bhai Sahib asked me to get something for him, not only had I not been able to find it, but he hadn't waited for me. But when I thought about the dream I began to understand its real meaning. A chocolate Easter egg is a thin layer of chocolate surrounding an empty space. I realized that what the teacher wanted was not the thin layer of chocolate but the empty space. An Easter egg is a pre-Christian symbol of rebirth. I had to learn to keep an empty inner space so that something within me could be born into consciousness.

INTROVERSION AND EMPTINESS

Turning inward, we still function responsibly in the outer world, but the focus of our attention has changed. Through meditation, aspiration, and inner work, the energy that used to flow into the outer world has been redirected inward where it purifies and transforms the psyche. Deep within us the whole psychic structure becomes reoriented away from the ego and towards the Self. This process of realignment is mostly hidden from the conscious mind, which could interfere and disturb the process. Dreams may tell us of the work that is taking place, encouraging us or pointing out aspects of the shadow or other inner work that may need our attention.

The alchemists called this stage of introversion "brooding," pointing to both the withdrawal of energy and the new life that will follow. We need to value this time of transition and not mistake it for depression or inertia. A fundamental change is taking place within us which needs most of our energy and attention. Our everyday outer life helps us not to become narcissistically involved with the inner changes. As the Sufis of

Nîshâpûr realized, the less we identify with our own transformation the less the ego is involved. Ego-identification with spiritual transformation can easily lead to inflation. Everyday life with all of its difficulties and problems keeps our feet on the ground and constantly reminds us that we are human.

Sometimes when people begin on the spiritual path they want to have a spiritually-oriented job or profession, to become a healer or therapist, for example. This is an understandable desire to express their spiritual nature in the outer world, but again points to an ego-identification with the quest. Spiritual life is about becoming nothing rather than becoming something. The wayfarer aspires to become empty so that she can be used. In the words of a Sufi prayer:

> I do not ask to see.
> I do not ask to know.
> I ask only to be used.

On the inner journey the patterns of ego-attachment dissolve through the energy of love. Allowing this dissolution to take place is a painful process of detachment; old values and identities fall away, leaving one empty and defenseless. The work of the wayfarer is to cooperate with this process and to resist the temptation to fill the emptiness with new attachments. Slowly, secretly, something comes alive within us, a new quality of life that is not focused on the ego but on the Self. What had been hidden deep within the heart becomes infused into consciousness. We begin to be permeated with the life of the spirit.

Almost imperceptibly, the stony road of desolation changes, and flowers appear. We are so conditioned to value only outer form that we do not notice the quality of our life changing. It is not the outer form of our life that changes, but its inner substance, as suggested by the Zen saying, "Before enlightenment, chop wood and carry water. After enlightenment, chop wood and carry water." What has happened is that we no longer see life solely from the limited perspective of the ego; the infinite eye of the heart begins to open. The outer picture remains the same but the inner experience is very different.

LOVE'S INTIMACY

Within the heart the mystery of His presence replaces the sorrow of His absence. Through our effort of perseverance, our devotion, and our disciplined practice of meditation, we prove to our Beloved that we are faithful and true. As we walk towards Him, often going one step backwards for every two we go forward, He comes to meet us. At first we do not notice, so great is the distance between us. But then one day we find that He is within our own heart. Without our knowing it, the dryness of the desert has opened us, has prepared the place for our meeting. In every human relationship, however close, however intimate, there are always two. When our Beloved comes to us we realize the overwhelming potency of this love affair in which there is only Oneness. He whom we love, whom we long for, is a part of our being. He kisses us on the inside of the heart, and in that moment all sense of desolation dissolves.

One kiss of the Beloved creates a sense of belonging that does not depend upon anything in the outer world. We know that we are loved and have found our real Home. This is the beginning of our spiritual unfolding in which we realize the real nature of love. What had been hidden in the depths begins to be glimpsed. We begin to taste the intoxicating wine known only to His lovers. For one more kiss we would sacrifice the whole world and our self.

Because He, the great artist, made us unique, for each of us this opening of the heart will be individual. Unannounced, like a thief in the night, He is suddenly present, removing the veil of separation. In this meeting there is no barrier of physical bodies or psychological problems. There is a melting in which we taste the secrets of our own inner self. We are awakened to the true touch of Him who will never betray us.

The first moment of this togetherness carries the infinite sweetness of a first love. What we have longed for is with us. Yet this moment of Oneness is only the beginning of the heart's expansion. Inner awakening is not a single moment of illumination, but a continuing widening of the horizon. Spiritual life is an unfolding into the infinite. Just as a child's horizon expands as it grows, so does the mystic's. For a child the whole world is at first the mother, then the house, then the neighborhood. Mystical awareness is a deepening perception of love's oneness, and, as Dhû'l-Nûn was told, "Love has no end because the Beloved has no end." The closeness and intimacy, the depth of love, continue to increase as the Beloved reveals to His lover aspects of His beauty and His majesty.

But there is a spiritual law that says we are never given these experiences for ourselves, only for others. After times of intimacy we return to the world, where we are able to bring a quality of remembrance into the world which is starving for such nourishment. We bring a fragrance of the beyond into our daily life where it resonates with those who need to be reminded of the infinite. In silence, heart speaks to heart. The heart that remembers His kiss shares its secret with others who need to know the truth of love's call. Sufis are known as doorkeepers of love, for through the open hearts of His lovers He nourishes His world with the "essence of the divine essence." Living our daily life in an attitude of service to Him whom we love, we help to keep the world attuned to love.

For the lover it can be painful to be thrown back into the outer world of separation after experiences of intimacy. When we know the sweetness of the Beloved's kiss, the world can appear empty and even desolate. What can we say of a bliss beyond reason and of an invisible lover? With our colleagues and family we have to remain silent, unable to openly share what is most precious. We know the illusion of the world but have to act our part in the play of life. We are His idiots, lost in an infinite ocean, and yet having to live in the constrictions of time and space.

Often when we first experience the wonder that is within us we long to tell others of the real miracle of being human. It can be painful to keep silent. But if we talk to those who are unresponsive, their doubts can affect us. Our new-found relationship with the beyond can be attacked by the negative thought-forms of others. This is the meaning of Christ's saying:

> Give not that which is holy unto the dogs, neither cast ye your pearls before swine, lest they trample them under their feet, and turn again and rend you.[9]

We live in a society which stresses material values and yet we know that they are insubstantial. This truth can be threatening to those who are not yet ready. We need

131

to learn to discriminate, as in the cartoon of the man tied up in a straitjacket who says to the mystic walking nearby, "How come I'm tied up in here and you're walking around free?" To which the mystic replies, "I knew who to say what to and you didn't." This is one of the reasons why a spiritual group is so valuable, for it is a space where we can openly share the heart's reality, the pain of separation and the ecstasy of nearness. Both in silence and in talking, the inner truth that is beyond all form is recognized and valued. The craziness of a quest that drives us into the empty unknown is accepted and understood.

In our everyday life we sometimes seem like strangers, travellers from another land. "Love is a stranger and speaks a strange language,"[10] and those who belong to Him carry His mark. Only those who have tasted love's wine can recognize the drunken look of another, know how nothing else but another sip will satisfy their longing. We belong to our Beloved and only He can fulfill us. This is the real patched frock of the Sufi, for "The reality of poverty is that one becomes rich through God alone."[11] In the world we feel the pull of ego and the senses and yet know that we have to look only to Him:

> We have to live our life in the world and be occupied with worldly affairs, and reach the highest stage in spite, or rather, because, of it. For the greater is the limitation, the greater will be the ultimate perfection by overcoming it.[12]

For the wayfarer the friction between the inner states and the pressures of outer life energizes the process of transformation. All energy is born from the tension of opposites, and even mundane experiences like financial worries can force one to make an effort and to try to reconcile the two worlds. We have to live the primal contradiction of incarnation: that we are both human and divine.

LIVING A GUIDED LIFE

Through inner experience we come to know our connection with the Divine. Working in the world, we have to trust this connection and bring its guidance into our outer life. One friend had a dream that described this process for her. She was naked in the marketplace. But then she was given a coat in whose pockets she found everything she needed. Naked and unprotected, in a state of surrender and poverty, we are inwardly dependent upon Him who alone can give us sustenance and protection. We fully realize the substance of this relationship when we live it out in the world, when we experience the wisdom and inner protection of the Self in our daily life. The alchemists called this stage the *rubedo*, the "reddening," because in order for an inner process to become fully alive it must have "blood," what the alchemists called the "redness" of life. Working in the world, we make real the inner connection of the heart and we bring the heart's remembrance into our everyday life. In the words of Abû Sa'îd ibn Abî 'l-Khayr:

> The true mystic goes in and out amongst the people and eats and sleeps with them and buys and sells in the market and marries and takes part in social intercourse, and never forgets God for a single moment.[13]

Through meditation and inner work we create an inner space that is unpolluted by the desires of the ego and the chatter of the mind. Going within the heart, we learn to listen to the voice of the Beloved, the guidance of the Self. However, it is not enough just to listen to His hint; we have to enact it. At first we will make many mistakes, sometimes following the voice of the ego or censoring the often irrational voice of the Self. But when we do not follow the prompting of the Self we may be left with a sense of a lost opportunity, or the feeling that we have let down the Self. When we do enact the heart's hint, we may glimpse through the effect of our actions the way the Self unfolds its mysterious purpose in the outer world. Gandhi, who said that he was guided, was once asked how he knew that he was guided by the Divine, because Hitler also said that he was guided. With his usual down-to-earth simplicity Gandhi replied, "You look at the results."

The higher Self speaks to us in different ways. For some it is a still, small voice, while for others an inner prompting or a feeling. We learn how it speaks to us, how this guidance often arrives unexpectedly without any relationship to the flow of our thoughts or feelings. Sometimes we can recognize the voice of the Self by its very incongruity. Enacting its message often achieves a result that we could not imagine. For example, following a feeling we go somewhere and find that we are in just the right place at the right time. Or we may get an inner prompting to say something to someone, and although the mind or our conditioning may try to censor it, we enact the prompting and then see how what we say unlocks a door within the other person or achieves an unexpected result. Once a friend was going to pick up her children from school and started a brief conversation with another mother in the school parking lot. The mother told her that she was suffering from a painful physical and psychological condition and didn't know what to do. To her own surprise my friend began to tell about the meditation of the heart that we practice. In the middle of the school parking lot she outlined the meditation, and at the same time was thinking that this was hardly the place to share something so sacred. But then the children came out of school and the conversation ended. That evening the mother rang her in deep gratitude saying that after she had gotten home and her children were busy she had gone to her room and tried the meditation. She immediately went off in meditation and the pain left her!

One of the fears that can hold us back from enacting the will of the Self is that of making mistakes, saying or doing things that are embarrassing or wrong. Of course we will make mistakes. But there is a spiritual law that we are always given an opportunity to correct a mistake—His mercy is always greater than His justice. We work for the will of the Beloved and are prepared to learn from any mistake that we may make. It is only the arrogance of the ego that is afraid of being wrong. My teacher said that she didn't mind anymore if she made a mistake because she was happy to apologize in humility. She had already lost everything and there was nothing left to lose. To fully accept that we are human is to accept that we will make mistakes, and the more we become immersed in the Self the less we care what others may think. We relate directly to the Beloved and not to the world's opinion.

An important aspect of following the will of the Self is not to try to improve upon its guidance. Then the ego interferes, thinking it knows better, and even with the best intentions we disturb the purpose of the Self. Working in the world, we need to step out of the way so that His will be done. We learn to trust our inner guidance and to discriminate between the voice of the ego and the voice of the Self. Eventually, without thought or hesitation, we instinctually enact the heart's prompting. The inner and outer world become bonded together as we unquestioningly follow the way of Khidr rather than the way of Moses.

WHERESOEVER YOU TURN, THERE IS THE FACE OF GOD

Due to His love, in the depths of our heart we come to know His Oneness. In meditation we glimpse behind the veil of multiplicity into the secret face of unity. The experience of Oneness is a central mystical experience in which the duality of lover and Beloved dissolves as something within us comes to know its real nature: there is nothing other than God. In the words of Ibn 'Arabî, "When you know yourself, your 'I-ness' vanishes and you know that you and God are one and the same."[14] In these moments we step out of the prison of the ego into the arena of the Self, into the deeper dimension of our own eternal being:

> When the mystery—of realizing that the mystic is one with the divine—is revealed to you, you will understand that you are no other than God and that you have continued and will continue ... without when and without times. Then you will see all your actions to be His actions and all your attributes to be His attributes and your essence to be His essence, though you do not thereby become He or He you, in either the greatest or the least degree. "Everything is perishing save

His Face," that is, there is nothing except His Face, "then, whithersoever you turn, there is the Face of God."[15]

Returning from meditation we find ourself back in duality and separation. For an infinite moment the ego was lost and we discovered our true being. But then the world closes around us, and in this world we need an ego. In moments of mystical ecstasy there is only Oneness and no sense of separation. We are both the vastness of the sky and the garbage on the street. You cannot live for long in this state. You need an ego to go shopping or to cook a meal. My teacher would sometimes be caught unexpectedly in a mystical state while out walking, and would not know who she was or where she lived. Then you have to wait for the mind and its boundaries to return.

The mystic has to learn how to live in the two worlds: to know the infinite inner oneness and yet to be able to live a balanced outer life. In our everyday life we are able to be guided by the Self, as a servant is guided by his master. But the ego still retains a sense of separate identity. We do not become God. The seventeenth-century Sufi, Sheikh Ahmad Sirhindî, stresses that after the stage of unity comes the stage of servanthood. We are His servants and the inner experience of unity helps us to more fully surrender ourselves so that His will can be done. Experiences of oneness finally break the grip of the ego. Because we know that we are in essence united with Him, we are able to serve Him more completely.

It is not easy to live with an awareness of the two worlds, because to have tasted Truth means to know the illusion of our everyday life. We have to be responsible in a world we *know* is not real. Our attention is often somewhere else, and we may at times have to force our attention back to this outer plane. When people have to drive home after our meditation meetings they need to remember to come right back into the physical plane, or their reactions may not be quite quick enough. I sometimes suggest that they listen to rock music, whose earthy beat can bring one back to this world, on their car radio.

Sufis need to be soldiers of the two worlds because we have to connect the inner and outer planes, and so bring the oneness of the heart into a world of multiplicity. Once the heart knows the secret of love's oneness, it carries this like a seed wherever it goes. It sings the song of unity and is an open door through which the energy of love can flow into the world. This love is not the *maya* of attachment but the power of remembrance which cuts away attachments and binds the creation back to the Creator. True love is the heart's affirmation that He is Lord. This love, which is at the axis of the world, "knits up reality and draws all things to their home in God."[16]

Bringing together the two worlds in our daily life, we suffer the pain of separation because it is His will. To quote al-Ghazzâlî:

> I want union with him and he wants separation;
> thus I leave what I want so that his wish comes
> true.[17]

But once we know the heart's secret of union we are no longer totally imprisoned within duality. A sense of oneness lies beneath the surface of consciousness. Even when the world seems empty of His presence we carry the heart's remembrance. More and more we come to see His hidden face within His creation:

> Rose and mirror and sun and moon
> > —what are they?
> Wherever we looked, there was always
> > Thy face.[18]

The eye of the heart sees behind the veil of appearances. The multiplicity of outer impressions is contained within a feeling of unity. The ego is held within the sphere of the Self, which gradually permeates all of our life with His presence. We no longer need to turn away from the world to seek Him because we have united the two worlds within us. In the words of Abû Sa'îd ibn Abî'l-Khayr, "Sufism consists of keeping the heart from anything that is not He. But there is not anything not He."[19]

"I was a Hidden Treasure. I longed to be known so I created the world."[20] Through coming to know Him we realize the deepest purpose of creation. Sufis are also known as "God's spies," because through the open eye of the heart He can see into His world. The eye which sees God is also the eye through which God sees the world. We are sent into the world where He wishes us to be, hidden under the cloak of ordinary life. Outwardly fitting into her worldly environment, the Sufi is inwardly free, being of use to her Beloved in whatever way He wills. We can be of service to our Lord in the world where He is forgotten, where His presence is unobserved. Individually, or as a group of lovers, we are an empty space through which His love can flow and His will can be enacted, often without our knowledge. The lover only seeks to be of service to her Beloved.

We belong to Him since before the beginning of time. We tasted the wine of union before the creation of the vine. In this world our work is to realize our

inner state of union and service and then to live it in
the world. Through this work we come to know His
presence and the truth of our non-existence:

> In the market, in the cloister—only God I saw.
> In the valley and on the mountain
> only God I saw.
> Him I have seen beside me oft in tribulation;
> In favor and in fortune—only God I saw.
> In prayer and in fasting,
> in praise and contemplation,
> In the religion of the Prophet
> only God I saw.
> Neither soul nor body, accident nor substance,
> Qualities nor causes—only God I saw.
> Like a candle I was melting in His fire;
> Amidst the flames outflashing
> only God I saw.
> Myself with mine own eyes I saw most clearly,
> But when I looked with God's eyes
> only God I saw.
> I passed away into nothingness, I vanished,
> And lo, I was the All-living—only God I saw.[21]

7. ABIDING IN GOD

Heaven and earth cannot contain Me,
but the heart of My devoted servant contains Me.

Hadîth qudsî

THE HEART'S SECRET

Love is the greatest power in the universe. The Sufi path uses the energy of love to cleanse the heart of impurities and turn it back to God. When the heart spins with love it can carry the human being beyond the horizons of the ego to where the mind cannot follow. To quote the Sufi master Bhai Sahib:

> We are simple people. But we can turn the heart
> of a human being so that the human being will go
> on and on, where nobody can even imagine it.[1]

Sufism is a science of love, for it understands how to use this energy to transform the wayfarer and send her Home. The Home we seek is not a place but a state of being in which the heart is aligned with God. The remembrance of God *is* this state of being when the inner awareness of the heart is a part of our conscious life. Reconnected to the source of our own Self, we hear the heart's continual affirmation that He is Lord. We are held in the presence of God.

We begin the quest with a longing for something we cannot name or place. The pain of the heart's awakening is the pain of awakening to our own forgetfulness. We begin to remember that we are exiles who have forgotten from whence we came. The heart holds the secrets of our origin, and yet the door of the heart is obscured by the ego and its desires. What we long for is so close and yet unobtainable, as Ibn 'Arabî expresses:

> ... God deposited within man knowledge of all things, then prevented him from perceiving what He had deposited within him.... This is one of the divine mysteries which reason denies and considers totally impossible. The nearness of this mystery to those ignorant of it is like God's nearness to His servant, as mentioned in His words, "We are nearer to him than you, but you do not see" (Qur'an 56:85), and His words, "We are nearer to him than his jugular vein" (50:16). In spite of this nearness, the person does not perceive and does not know.... No one knows what is within himself until it is unveiled instant by instant.[2]

The work of purification, confronting the shadow and the attachments of the ego, prepares us for this "unveiling." Inner work takes us deep within to the root of the root of our being. Then we can stand on the rock of the Self, without which we would become unbalanced by the slightest glimpse of what is hidden behind the veils of separation.

What stands between the wayfarer and her divine nature is the ego, the "I." Bâyezîd Bistâmî saw his Lord in a dream and asked, "How am I to find you?" He replied, "Leave yourself and come!" The wayfarer's own self, her personal identity, is the illusion that separates her from her goal. We are the barrier between lover and Beloved. This simple but paradoxical reality is the basis of *fanâ*, the annihilation of the lover that leads to union with the Beloved:

> Listen, riffraff:
>> Do you want to be ALL?
> Then go,
>> go and become NOTHING.[3]

To become nothing, to "die before you die," is the only solution to the pain of separation. What we think we are has to be burnt in the pain of longing, destroyed in the fire of love. When Irina Tweedie returned to the West after the death of her sheikh, friends who knew that she had been with a great master asked her what it was like. She replied, "It was like being run over by a steamroller." The Sufi path is a journey of self-destruction, which is why the teacher sometimes carries the title of executioner. As long as the ego rules the human being, there can be no lasting experience of the Self. Two cannot live in one heart; either the ego or the Self must go.

The ego has to get out of the way in order for the seeker to realize the truth of love's union. But it does not want to surrender its position and power, and will fight with all its strength, trickery, and powers of illusion. We need to persevere and keep the heart's desire burning, and still it is not enough. Alone we cannot go beyond the ego. Alone we cannot renounce our own self. This is why we need a teacher and a spiritual tradition to hold us while we make this transition. The grace of God that flows through a spiritual tradition breaks the patterns of attachment while holding us Somewhere. We are held in the heart of God as He takes us Home.

We have to make every effort, but without His grace all our efforts would be useless because we would still be caught in the ego. There comes the time when we have to give up even the desire to progress, even the desire to get closer to Him whom we love. We have to surrender every effort in order to be taken by God to God. In the words of Abû'l Hasan Kharaqânî:

> He who says he has attained God, has not,
> While he who says he has been taken to God
> Has indeed attained union with God.

What we most want we cannot find, but we have to seek with every effort until we surrender. Then in the act of surrender we create an inner space for the Beloved to reveal Himself. We die to our own desire, even the desire for Truth, and then Truth reveals Itself. The eye of the heart opens and we see that there is nothing other than God.

The process of dying is a slow and gradual work. Slowly the ego dies as attachments and conditioning fall away. With each little death a veil falls away and the horizon of the Self expands. After these moments of expansion there is usually a period of contraction as we integrate our new-found awareness, learn to live with a wider perspective. Slowly, almost imperceptibly, the focus of our awareness shifts from the ego to the Self. As this happens the rate of expansion, the speed of the journey, intensifies. Faster and faster we flow with the currents of love which carry us Home.

The dissolution of the ego unites us with the Self. What was always present but hidden comes to the surface. The all-knowing and all-seeing Substance within the heart permeates consciousness with Its presence.

We continue to live our ordinary, everyday life, but we begin to feel that it is included within something greater, something which does not belong to the mind or the personality. When He wills we can have access to this other dimension within us. The ego cannot reach the Self, but once we learn to surrender, the Self can reach us. The ego and the mind instinctively step aside and we are in the presence of what is eternal.

FANÂ AND BAQÂ

For the Sufi there are three journeys: the journey from God, the journey to God, and the journey in God. The journey from God is the soul's journey into the world, when, born into a body, we forget our essential state of union with God. The ego covers the memory of wholeness with its sense of a separate identity. We become enslaved to the ego with its desires and demands, and are securely caught in the illusions of the world. Then, in a moment of grace, we are awakened. The soul's memory of union ignites the fire of longing, and we begin the long, laborious journey Homeward. Turning away from the outer world and the constrictive desires of the ego, we look inward, attracted by His hidden presence within the heart.

The journey to God is the process of *fanâ*, the annihilation of the ego. The ego and its dark twin, the shadow, need to be removed from their position at the center of life's stage. Through love, devotion, and the help of the teacher and the path, the ego loses its stranglehold as we sense a deeper and more enduring identity. Learning to surrender, we acknowledge something greater than our individual self. We begin to taste the freedom that comes from servitude, a freedom far beyond the ego's notion of autonomy. But this work of dissolving the grip of the ego carries the pain of crucifixion, as in the Persian saying, "The ego will not go with laughter or with caresses. It must be chased in sorrow and drowned in tears."

Turning away from the world and turning back to God require the greatest effort. To remember Him whom we had forgotten carries the agony of crucifixion as we are torn between the ego and the Self. We have to stay true to the heart's longing despite the doubts and confusions of the mind. We are tortured by our own weaknesses and deceived by our own strengths. Everything has to be given up as we step into the nothingness of love. But in the midst of our despair something is born and grows silently within us. Nourished by devotion and His love, the child of Truth opens its eyes. This is the inner eye of the heart, as expressed in the famous *hadîth qudsî*, "My servant ceases not to draw nigh unto Me by works of devotion, until I love him, and when I love him I am the eye by which he sees and the ear by which he hears."

What is born within the wayfarer is a state of being which is an inner awareness of His presence. The ego will always exist in a state of separation, because the very nature of the ego is its sense of having a separate identity. But within the heart, the Self, His divine consciousness, is awakened to His eternal presence. In the words of Ibn 'Arabî,

> By Himself He sees Himself, and by Himself He knows Himself. None sees Him other than He, and none perceives Him other than He.[4]

Through surrender and devotion the wayfarer *participates* in His knowledge of Himself. The mind and the ego can never grasp an experience of total unity in which there is no distinction between observer and observed, but the heart's experience of His unity is reflected into our ordinary consciousness. Something within us knows that He is present.

When the ego steps aside the real spiritual journey begins, the journey in God. Our state of surrender allows us to experience our deepest nature, in which we are eternally united with God. The state of union begins to unfold dynamically within the wayfarer. *Fanâ* is the annihilation of the ego that leads to *baqâ*, abiding in God, also known as "abiding after passing away." The experience of union with God is not the end of the journey, but the beginning of a new life in which the mystic becomes more and more deeply immersed in His presence, more and more lost in God.

ABIDING IN EMPTINESS

Baqâ is a co-existing state of separation and union. Living in the outer world and functioning through the ego, we know separation. But within the heart He whom we love is present. Once we have surrendered to the intensity of love's union, even His apparent absence is a sign of His presence. To quote al-Hallâj, "If He hides His presence from you it is because He is listening to you."[5]

We know that we can never know Him. We understand that we do not understand. But we are a part of the mystery of His revealing Himself to Himself. He whom we love is beyond form, beyond knowledge, beyond the mind's limited horizon. To live in the presence of God is to be contained within a presence of non-existence. Ruthlessly we are presented with our own inability to come close to Him or to keep distant from Him, for, in the words of the *hadîth*, "The heart of the faithful is held between the two fingers of the All-merciful. He turns it wherever He wills."

To be surrendered to God is to give ourself into unknowingness, into a space beyond thought or form. His presence then comes into our life in many forms, as a companion, as inner guidance, as a sweetness suddenly felt. And underneath all of His manifestations is a deepening communion with what can never be manifest, with an emptiness, a nothingness, "the dark silence in which all lovers lose themselves."[6] This silence is the real Home of the mystic, where we inwardly abide with God.

In this inner silence, love reveals its secret potency, an unending expansion of the heart. The path of love reveals its power only when there is no one there to interfere, when all sense of identity has been merged, dissolved "like sugar in water." In meditation the ego and the mind are left behind and the inner chamber of the heart opens and opens. The heart of hearts is the place and the state of union, the timeless moment in which we are taken by God to God. This is the deepest fulfillment of being human, in which His hidden secret becomes known to Himself:

> Man is My secret and I am his secret. The inner knowledge of the spiritual essence is a secret of My secrets. Only I put this into the heart of My good servant, and none may know his state other than Me.[7]

THE SYSTEM

For centuries the Sufi masters have known the science
of love and guided their disciples through the stages
of the way that leads from the isolation of the ego to
the further shores of the heart. They have developed
a subtle and exact system to transform the psyche and
the substance of the heart, pushing the wayfarer to
the limits of endurance in order to prepare her for her
Beloved.

They work in harmony with the inner energies
and the individual disposition of the disciple, invisibly
holding her within the tradition. The teacher holds the
disciple within his heart, just as the teacher is held within
the heart of his teacher, even if his teacher is no longer
physically alive. The transmission of the path, the chain
of spiritual superiors, is a containment in love. This
dynamic container provides the security that enables
the wayfarer to walk into the fire of *fanâ*, the self-
destruction that brings her to realize her own unique
nearness to God—the closeness of the soul to the
source.

The Sufi path is a system designed to take souls
Home to God. Most of the work of transformation is
hidden from the wayfarer, but over the years tremendous
inner changes take place. The mental, psychological,
spiritual, and even physical structure of the wayfarer
is changed, as one friend was shown in a prophetic
dream in which he saw his body changing into a
human heart. In this dream his heart travelled through
space, turning inside and out, never missing a beat.
As it turned, the cells of his body changed into blue
and gold musical notes, until the whole of his body
was composed of blue and gold notes. As the process
progressed his body became more and more formless
until it was just a blue and gold glow.

The transformation of the inner structure of the wayfarer is necessary if we are to be able to experience the higher vibrations of the Self without becoming unbalanced. Spiritual life is a question of speed. The inner dimensions of the Self spin at a faster frequency than the dense material plane, and someone unprepared could easily be thrown off balance. Not only is the wayfarer exposed to a reality that is nothingness to the mind, the abyss of divine non-being, but this nothingness is highly dynamic. The further we travel into the heart the faster spins the energy of love. We need to become attuned to these frequencies and develop a finer psychic and physical body through which these energies can flow.

Without the guidance of the sheikh and the grace of the tradition, the inner opening of the wayfarer could be too sudden, her inner structure unprepared. Then the faster energies would hit against the denser structure rather than flow through. The result could easily be physical discomfort or psychological instability. There is even the danger of psychosis if the energy of the beyond smashes against a mind that has not surrendered. But on the Sufi path the wayfarer is contained in love and looked after by a succession of the friends of God. This is beautifully imaged in a dream in which the wayfarer is held in an embrace by his teacher:

> My teacher looks in my eyes and then suddenly gives me a big hug. My head lies on her heart and I feel as if I am relaxing safely on a big rock amidst crashing waves. At the same time I feel as if I would fall into an endless abyss. Then my teacher says, "With all my love and the blessings of my teacher, Bhai Sahib. And now we go to eat."

For centuries, wayfarers have been walking this intoxicating path of transformation. Following their footsteps we each make our own sacrifice and realize our own relationship to Him whom our heart loves. The path belongs to Him because, in the words of Maghribî, "Whoever goes to His street goes with His feet." He guides back to His light whom He will, and His friends help Him in this work. Creating a space where the energies of love flow into the world, His lovers are a beacon of light pointing out the inner path within the heart. Those whose heart resonates with this frequency of love are attracted to the path. Some come to a Sufi group for a while to help them on their way. Others come and stay forever, finding an inner bond and spiritual companionship that fulfill a deep need.

The pathway to the beyond is a thin thread easily overlooked or lost amidst the clamor of the world. But in the companionship of friends we become attuned or focused in a manner that helps us to see this thread, to grasp its immense significance, and to allow it to guide us. A Sufi master once gave a precious stone to a prospective disciple and told him to take it to the market and have it valued by the stall holders. The disciple returned and said that it had been valued at a hundred gold pieces. The sheikh then told him to take this same stone to the jewellers' quarter in the city, and again have it valued. When the disciple returned he told the sheikh that the jewellers had valued the stone at over a thousand gold pieces. The sheikh said, "They are the experts and know what the stone is really worth." His lovers know the value of their own connection to Him, and this resonates in the atmosphere of the group. The hearts of those who have paid the price of love silently speak of the wonder of the journey.

THE NEED OF THE TIME

Sufism is the ancient wisdom of the heart. Like a stream which goes underground and then reappears, this wisdom is always present in the world, sometimes visible and sometimes hidden. Some great Sufis have been public figures; many have worked in the disguise of ordinary men and women. They belong to God and respond to the need of the time. At the present time in the West there is a need for this path of the heart to be made known, for this ancient tradition to be made more accessible.

In our Western world there is a hunger for the wisdom and nourishment that come from the inner world. In dreams, visions, and the silence of longing, the inner journey awakens within us and we are called back "to the root of the root of our own self." Yet our culture has forgotten the way of the mystic, which is so at variance with the rational and material values that surround us. There appear to be few signposts to guide the traveller, who is so often left stranded, confusing longing with depression, or believing that the desire for God is just an inability to adjust to the real world.

In this century, psychology and the many different forms of therapy have helped us to understand the dynamics of the unconscious. We are beginning to learn about the healing and transformation that can come from within. Psychology is a valuable contemporary science, but the mystic has different intentions from those who seek psychological healing or the resolution of problems. The heart's desire for union with God activates a process of psychological ego-destruction that is both terrifying and intoxicating. The mystic does not seek ego-fulfillment, but to be lost in the abyss of nothingness. At the same time we need to live a balanced life and not allow the contents of the unconscious to overwhelm us. The Sufi path has explored and documented the psychological and spiritual unfolding that belongs to the journey Home. This wisdom is valuable not only to those who follow the Sufi path, but to others who need to understand the processes of transformation that belong to the mystical journey.

The wayfarer follows love's call, like the moth drawn to the flame of annihilation. At the same time the Sufi lives an everyday life in the world. We have to learn to live in the two worlds, to have both feet firmly on the ground and yet with our head to support the sky. Living in the two worlds is an integral part of the Sufi tradition. The subtle balance of inner and outer states, the integration of the spiritual and everyday life, belongs to the wisdom of this path.

Understanding how to balance the two worlds, how to live a spiritual life within a material culture, is valuable to many contemporary seekers. The pressures and demands of everyday life make it difficult to retire from the world. The path of the *sannyasin*, the wandering monk who has renounced the world, is far easier in the East than in the West. One friend who had lived as a monk in Thailand for many years returned to Washington, D.C., to discover that the only places where his begging bowl would be filled were the Thai and Sri Lankan embassies!

Living in both realms—working in the world, having a family, while at the same time realizing the Truth—is a cornerstone of the Sufi path. The inner and outer world, the heart's secrets and the most ordinary things, combine to create the necessary conditions for the path. The friction between the two worlds wears away the ego, which is unable to contain the seeming contradiction of the endless inner expansion and the limitations of everyday life. The prison of our temporal home contains the key of the heart's freedom. Here lies the secret alchemy of the Sufi path.

For centuries, Sufi masters have led their disciples through a path of inner experiences, even as the disciples lived an ordinary outer life. The combination of the inner and outer worlds produces a powerful dynamic that helps the wayfarer to realize her true nature. Remembering God in our daily life, we bring the imprint of the soul into the world of time and space. Only within the heart can we contain the most primal pair of opposites, that we are at the same time divine, immortal spirits and temporal creatures. The tension between our divine and human natures produces the longing that burns us and takes us Home.

Inwardly looking towards God, we learn to live our devotion not as some idealized state, but as a center of stillness and love within the limitations and difficulties of the world. We do not reject His creation but rather come to know its deeper purpose, as a reflection of His Oneness. When we love Him in the midst of the world, amidst our mundane, everyday life, we realize this hidden secret of creation—"in everything there is a sign, a clue to 'He is One.'"[8]

The way of the Sufi is to contain duality within the oneness of love. We are both separate and united with Him whom we love. *Lâ ilâha illâ 'llah* ("There is no god but God") turns us away from the world and back to God. But in the affirmation of His Oneness we realize that there is nothing other than God. Surrendering to the pain of separation we experience love's deeper truth in which only the Beloved exists:

all the world's lows
and highs are You:
I know not what You are
but You are everything.[9]

APPENDIX

SYMBOLS EXPERIENCED
IN MEDITATION AND VISIONS[1]

Symbols experienced in meditation and visions can have important spiritual significance, although they are not yet the Truth. These symbols generally have a different symbolic meaning from dream images.

ARROW: Powers which long to reach the target.

BELL RINGING: Sign of progress on the path.

BIRD: A symbol of the soul, the power of your soul.

BOW AND ARROW: The power which comes to you to enable you to reach the goal.

BUFFALO: Dark forces within the unconscious.

CALF, WHITE: Clear, pure consciousness, innocence.

CHALICE, GOLDEN: Self-realization.

COLORS:

BLOOD RED: Sensuality.

BLUE: It could be the higher mind, but different blues have different meanings.

DIAMOND BLUE: Higher mind.

LAVENDER BLUE: Intuitional mind.

OCEAN BLUE: Spiritual consciousness.

DIAMOND WHITE: The highest feminine principle—the Great Mother—at its most intensive.

GREEN: Different meanings—life energy, movement, activity, joy of living, self-realization, and peace.

PURPLE: The power of life.

RED, DIFFERENT REDS TOGETHER: Consciousness of the physical plane.

CRANE, WHITE: A sign of coming happiness.

CROSS: Threefold symbol of being: transcendental, universal, and individual.

CROWN: Fulfillment now or later. It could be a prophetic vision when you see it on your own head.

CUBE, BLACK: The Kaaba in Mecca.

DAWN: An opening, the beginning of something new which has not quite arrived.

DEER: Swiftness on the path, progress made on the path.

DELICATE COLORS AND FLOWERS: A sign that your spiritual practices have a result. They signify the opening of consciousness.

DONKEY: An obstacle, especially a donkey that goes backwards.

DRAGON: Worldly power, ego, little self.

FIRE: Usually big emotions or dramas, family problems.

FLUTE: The call to understanding, perhaps an announcement or an inner victory. If you suddenly hear or see a flute or an ear it has the same meaning.

FRUIT: The result of our efforts in meditation.

GREY ZONE: This is the level on which magicians and witches work. Sometimes on falling asleep or when you are utterly peaceful you can tune into it. Carl Jung called these hypnagogic visions. These visions have meaning for the person who sees them but they are usually very personal.

HORSE: Especially a galloping horse: power, energy, passion. If you see a horse in meditation be careful, look out!

HUMMING (AS OF BEES OR FLIES): Opening of the brow *chakra*.

JOURNEYS: In trains or cars, signifies movement and progress in life. Journeys on board a ship are always progress in the spiritual path.

JUNGLE OR FOREST: Unconscious.

LIGHT: Light is always a power or different powers.

> BLUISH, ULTRAVIOLET LIGHT: The color of *prana*.

> DARK RED LIGHT: This is the light of the lowest earthly plane and it comes to the earthly plane to change completely. It is the greatest power of change and has the greatest dynamism.

> GOLDEN LIGHT: The highest wisdom.

> RED GOLDEN LIGHT: Forces in the process of change.

> SUNLIGHT: The light of Truth.

> WHITE LIGHT: The archetypal feminine. Your mother or the consciousness of God in your mother. Great love for the mother.

> LIGHT AROUND US: A sign of progress. If the light comes from above, it shows that a great power is coming either from God or your guru. Sometimes we see the light between the eyebrows or sometimes it comes from the left and we can only see it out of the corner of our eye. The color of the light has a significance, and the feeling quality is important: it makes a difference whether you are afraid or not.

MILK: The knowledge and power of the Divine. It is considered to be flowing out of the consciousness of the Divine.

MOON: Feminine spirituality, bliss, and the power of vision.

MOUNTAIN: Climbing a mountain is a symbol of your life cycle, your consciousness. It is the road leading upwards to the Divine.

PRIMAL SCREAM OR CRY: The cry of our inner energy wanting to be free.

PYRAMID: Longing.

RAIN: Grace of God falling on you.

RIVER: Flow of life, the river of life, the movement in your consciousness.

RED ROSE(S): Surrender.

WHITE ROSE(S): Absolute pure spiritual surrender.

RUBIES OR RED DIAMONDS: The color of the earthly plane. It could also be the consciousness of the mother at the lowest physical level.

SCORPION: Very bad energies or people who are trying to attack you with their energy. Not a good sign.

SNAKE: *Kundalini* or a symbol of danger from the unconscious, especially if it's green. It could be bad energy, not necessarily in you.

OUROBOROS (THE SNAKE EATING ITS TAIL): Cosmic creation.

WHITE SNAKE: A cosmic snake.

SNOW: Condition of purity, peace, and silence. If you see flowers coming out of the snow you are at the beginning of a new life.

SPINNING CIRCLE OR DISC: The power in becoming.

SWAN: A soul which is already freed, a realized soul.

TEETH FALLING OUT: Fixed conditioning or ideas are suddenly or gradually disappearing, patterns of thinking are falling away.

TREE: The picture of life, the life power, the tree of life.

UNKNOWN FACES: Real spiritual beings.

WATER: A condition, a plane of consciousness.

The objects which you see with closed eyes in meditation are formed on the mental field of energy. Our mind creates any object from its substance. The mind is a reality. It has a kind of matter from which objects are created. The objects, thought-forms, that you create on the mental plane don't disappear. They remain on the mental plane but our state of consciousness changes and we don't see them anymore. The thought-forms remain in the atmosphere.

NOTES

INTRODUCTION

1. Quoted by A. J. Arberry, *The Doctrine of the Sufis*, p. 152.
2. Told in *Daughter of Fire*, by Irina Tweedie, pp. 382-3.
3. Quoted by al-Qushayrî, *Principles of Sufism*, p. 330.
4. Quoted by Cyril Glassé, *The Concise Encyclopedia of Islam*, p. 150.
5. Told by Farîd ud-Dîn 'Attâr, *Muslim Saints and Mystics*, p. 47.
6. Quoted by Annemarie Schimmel, *Mystical Dimensions of Islam*, p. 40.
7. Ibid., p. 43.
8. Told by 'Attâr, *Muslim Saints and Mystics*, p. 98.
9. Quoted by R.S. Bhatnagar, *Dimensions of Classical Sufi Thought*, p. 58.
10. Ibid., p. 58.
11. Quoted by Stephen Mitchell, *The Enlightened Mind*, p. 75.
12. Quoted by Schimmel, p. 50.
13. Quoted by Bhatnagar, p. 57.
14. Quoted by Schimmel, p. 58.
15. Quoted by Bhatnagar, p. 65.
16. Quoted by Louis Massignon, *The Passion of al-Hallâj*, vol. 3, p. 47.
17. Quoted by Schimmel, p. 43.
18. Quoted by Bhatnagar, p. 54.
19. Ibid., p. 53.
20. Ibid., p. 75.
21. Quoted by Nicholson, *Studies in Islamic Mysticism*, p. 52.
22. *The Secrets of God's Mystical Oneness*, trans. John O'Kane, p. 533.
23. Quoted by Bhatnagar, p. 80.
24. Ibid., p. 82.
25. "Whoso Knoweth Himself," from the *Treatise on Being* (*Risale-t-ul-wujudiyyah*), pp. 3-4.
26. Quoted by Bhatnagar, p. 92.
27. Quoted by Schimmel, p. 266.
28. Glassé, pp. 167-8.
29. Quoted by Eva de Vitray-Meyerovitch, *Rûmî and Sufism*, p. 24.

30. Trans. John Moyne and Coleman Barks, *Open Secret*, p. 8.
31. *Rubai'yât,* "Quatrains," quoted by de Vitray-Meyerovitch, p. 107.
32. Trans. Andrew Harvey, *Love's Fire: Recreations of Rumi*, p. 105.
33. Schimmel, p. 255.
34. Ibid., p. 240.
35. *Mathnawî,* trans. Coleman Barks, *This Longing*, p. 20.
36. Ibid., p. 21.

1. THE LONGING OF THE HEART

1. Quoted by Schimmel, p. 133.
2. Persian song, quoted by Tweedie, p. 87.
3. 'Abd al-Qâdir al-Jîlânî, *The Secret of Secrets*, trans. Shaykh Tosun Bayrak, p. 39.
4. Trans. Charles Upton, *Doorkeeper of the Heart*, p. 28.
5. Trans. Annemarie Schimmel, *The Triumphal Sun*, p. 210.
6. Al-Junayd.
7. Quoted by Schimmel, p. 293.
8. Quoted by William Chittick, *The Sufi Path of Love*, p. 339.
9. Quoted by Tweedie, p. 135.
10. Ibn al-Fârid, Khamriyya, the "Wine Ode," R. A. Nicholson, *Studies in Islamic Mysticism*, p. 184.
11. Maghribî, quoted by Cyprian Rice, *The Persian Sufis*, p. 79.
12. Told by Schimmel, p. 45.
13. Trans. Daniel Liebert, *Rumi: Fragments, Ecstasies*, 22.
14. Francis Thompson, *The Hound of Heaven*, ll. 1-5.
15. *St. Mark* 15:34.
16. Told in *For the Love of the Dark One: Songs of Mirabai*, trans. Andrew Schelling, p. 22.
17. *Song of Songs*, 5:2, 5:5.
18. Quoted by Claude Addas, *Quest for the Red Sulphur: The Life of Ibn 'Arabî*, p. 61.
19. *Principles of Sufism*, p. 343.
20. Abû Sa'îd al-Kharrâz, quoted in *The Abode of Spring*, p. 191.
21. Abû Nu'aym al-Isfahânî, quoted by Schimmel, p. 132.
22. Quoted by Massignon, vol. 1, p. 606.
23. Quoted by Schimmel, p. 139.
24. Najm al-Dîn Kubrâ, quoted by Henry Corbin, *The Man of Light in Iranian Sufism*, pp. 72-3.

25. Shâh Ne'matollah, quoted by Peter Lamborn Wilson and Nasrollah Pourjavady, *The Drunken Universe*, p. 111.
26. Rûmî, trans. Andrew Harvey, *Love's Fire: Recreations of Rumi*, p. 77.

2. SUFI PRACTICES: THE DHIKR & MEDITATION

1. *Sûra* 6:91.
2. Quoted by R. A. Nicholson, *Studies in Islamic Mysticism*, p. 7.
3. 'Abd al-Qâdir al-Jîlânî, p. 45.
4. Schimmel, p. 169.
5. Peter Lamborn Wilson and Nasrollah Pourjavady, *The Drunken Universe*, p. 45.
6. Lao Tsu, *Tao Te Ching*, trans. Gia-Fu Feng and Jane English, p. 1.
7. The Blessed John Ruysbroeck, *The Adornment of the Spiritual Marriage*, quoted by F. C. Happold, *Mysticism*, p. 293.
8. Jîlî, quoted by Nicholson, *Studies in Islamic Mysticism,* p. 93.
9. Qur'an 2:109.
10. Quoted by Nicholson, *The Mystics of Islam*, p. 113.
11. Quoted by Massignon, vol. 3, p. 42.
12. Abû Sa'îd al-Kharrâz, quoted by al-Qushayrî, p. 274.
13. Told by 'Attâr, *Muslim Saints and Mystics*, p. 47.
14. The bliss of sexual orgasm is the one common experience of the bliss of the Self, given to humanity for the sake of procreation.
15. Quoted by Bhatnagar, p. 48.
16. 'Attâr, *The Conference of the Birds*. trans. C.S. Nott, p. 102.
17. Tweedie, pp. 821-2.
18. Mahmûd Shabistarî, quoted by Bhatnagar, p. 118.
19. Al-Qushayrî, p. 159.
20. *Dhyana* and *samadhi* are Sanskrit forms describing states of meditation.
21. Tweedie, unpublished lecture, "The Paradoxes of Mysticism," Wrekin Trust, "Mystics and Scientists Conference," 1985.
22. "Burnt Norton," ll. 42-3, *Four Quartets.*
23. *The Tempest*, iv.i. 146-7.
24. Quoted by Bhatnagar, p. 147.
25. Mahmûd Shabistarî, quoted by Bhatnagar, p. 116.

3. POLISHING THE MIRROR OF THE HEART

1. Irina Tweedie, *Daughter of Fire*, p. x.
2. *The Way of Individuation*, pp. 108-9.
3. *Collected Works*, vol. 13, para. 335.
4. *Psalms* 118:22.
5. *The Psychology of the Transference*, p. 34.
6. *Katha Upanishad*, Bk. II.1.
7. Quoted by Jung, *Collected Works*, vol. 13, para. 292. Jung refers to the parable of the unjust steward (*St. Luke* 16:1-8) as an example of using the shadow consciously.
8. Alchemical text, quoted by Jung, *Collected Works*, vol. 12, para. 434.
9. *Hadîth qudsî.*
10. Rûmî, quoted by Connie Zweig and Jeremiah Abrams, *Meeting the Shadow*, p. 80.
11. *Knowing Woman*, p. 76.
12. For the full text of the dream see Vaughan-Lee, *Catching the Thread*, p. 107.
13. For the full text of the dream and interpretation see Vaughan-Lee, *The Lover and the Serpent*, pp. 86-90.
14. C. G. Jung, quoted by Miguel Serrano, *C. G. Jung and Hermann Hesse*, p. 60.
15. E. Edinger, *The Anatomy of the Psyche*, p. 6.
16. *The Conference of the Birds*, p. 132, author's italics.

4. DREAMWORK

1. *Psychological Reflections*, p. 53.
2. Ibid., p. 72.
3. J. C. Cooper, *An Illustrated Encyclopaedia of Traditional Symbols* (London: Thames and Hudson, 1978) is an excellent book on symbolism.
4. *Man and His Symbols*, p. 96.
5. An excellent book that offers practical guidance for both active imagination and dreamwork is *Innerwork* by Robert Johnson (San Francisco: Harper and Row, 1986).
6. See Henry Corbin, *Creative Imagination in the Sufism of Ibn 'Arabî.*

7. See Vaughan-Lee, *In the Company of Friends*, pp. 43-9, "The Attitude Necessary for Inner Work." The African tale of the girl and her necklace tells the same archetypal story.

8. For the complete text and interpretation of the dream see Vaughan-Lee, *The Lover and the Serpent*, pp. 121-3.

9. *Hadîth qudsî* (extra-Qur'anic revelation), quoted by Schimmel, *Mystical Dimensions of Islam*, p. 133.

10. Told in *Daughter of Fire*, p. 157.

11. Rûmî, *Rubai'yât*, "Quatrains," quoted by de Vitray-Meyerovitch, p. 106.

12. *Sufi Symbolism*, ed. Javad Nurbakhsh, vols. I-VI, gives an explanation of many Sufi symbols, some of which are relevant to dreamwork. The author's books, *The Lover and the Serpent*, *Catching the Thread*, *The Bond with the Beloved*, and *In the Company of Friends*, explore the meaning of some symbols as they appear in specific dreams.

13. Lâhijî, quoted by Corbin, *The Man of Light in Iranian Sufism*, p. 118.

14. *Psychological Reflections*, p. 74.

15. For a complete interpretation of the dream, see Vaughan-Lee, *Catching the Thread*, pp. 197-203.

16. Tweedie, *Daughter of Fire*, p. 220.

17. *Psychological Reflections*, p. 64.

18. James Hillman, *Insearch*, p. 63.

19. The dynamic of transference, as, for example, the therapist becoming a father- or mother-figure to the client, is often an important part of this sense of security.

5. THE RELATIONSHIP WITH THE TEACHER

1. *Mathnawî,* I, 2, l. 943-5, quoted by de Vitray-Meyerovitch, p. 117.

2. *St. John* 20:16.

3. See Vaughan-Lee, *Catching the Thread*, p. 209.

4. Claude Addas, *Quest for the Red Sulphur*, p. 36.

5. Persian song, quoted by Tweedie, p. 87.

6. *The Secret of God's Mystical Oneness*, pp. 491-3.

7. *The Sufi Message of Hazrat Inayat Khan*, vol. X, p. 65.

8. Quoted by Alexander Lipski, *Life and Teachings of Anandamayi Ma*, p. 50.

9. Najm al-Dîn Kubrâ, quoted by Corbin, *The Man of Light in Iranian Sufism*, pp. 72-3.
10. Qur'an, "Light *Sûra*" (24:35).
11. Quoted by J. G. Bennett, *The Masters of Wisdom*, p. 180.
12. Rûmî, *Mathnawî*, IV, 1. 2138-48, trans. R. A. Nicholson, *Rïmî, Poet and Mystic*, p. 87.
13. *C. G. Jung, Emma Jung, Toni Wolf: A Collection of Remembrances*, pp. 51-2.
14. Tweedie, p. 149.
15. Trans. John Moyne and Coleman Barks, *Open Secret*, p. 21.
16. "Tested with Fire and Spirit," unreleased video interview, June 1988.
17. *Walad-Nâma*, quoted by Eva de Vitray-Meyerovitch, *Rûmî and Sufism*, p. 28.
18. See Introduction, pp. 6, 22-5.
19. Bhai Sahib, quoted by Tweedie, p. 144.
20. Told by 'Attâr, *Muslim Saints and Mystics*, pp. 208-9.
21. Rûmî, trans. Coleman Barks, *One-Handed Basket Weaving*, p. 80.
22. Al-Hallâj, quoted by Massignon, vol. 1, p. 614.
23. Jîlî, quoted by Corbin, *Spiritual Body and Celestial Earth*, p. 159.
24. Kalâbâdhî, quoted by Bhatnagar, p. 71.

6. UNITING THE TWO WORLDS

1. Quoted by Nicholson, *Studies in Islamic Mysticism*, p. 55.
2. Quoted by Shâfi'î, *Freedom from the Self*, p. 213.
3. Adapted from *The Conference of the Birds*, pp. 87-8.
4. Ibn 'Arabî, quoted by Bhatnagar, pp. 89-90.
5. Told by J. G. Bennett, *The Masters of Wisdom*, p. 180.
6. *St. Luke* 17:21.
7. Quoted by Schimmel, p. 146.
8. Rûmî, translated by Daniel Liebert, *Rumi: Fragments, Ecstasies*, p. 21.
9. *St. Matthew* 7:6.

10. Rûmî, trans. Kabir Helminski, *Love is a Stranger*, p. 18.
11. Yahyâ ibn Ma'âdh, quoted by Nurbakhsh, p. 15.
12. Bhai Sahib, quoted by Tweedie, p. 387.
13. Quoted by Nicholson, *Studies in Islamic Mysticism*, p. 55.
14. Quoted by Bhatnagar, p. 92.
15. Ibn 'Arabî, quoted by Bhatnagar, p. 92.
16. Evelyn Underhill, *Mysticism*, p. 130.
17. Quoted by Schimmel, *Mystical Dimensions of Islam*, p. 135.
18. Mîr, Ibid., p. 289.
19. *The Secret of God's Mystical Oneness*, p. 367.
20. *Hadîth qudsî*.
21. Bâbâ Kûhî, quoted by Bhatnagar, pp. 151-2.

7. ABIDING IN GOD

1. Tweedie, p. 537.
2. Quoted by Chittick, *The Sufi Path of Knowledge*, p. 154.
3. Fakhruddîn 'Irâqî, *Divine Flashes*, trans. William Chittick and Peter Lamborn Wilson, p. 78.
4. *Whoso Knoweth Himself*, p. 4.
5. Quoted by Massignon, vol. 3, p. 131.
6. The Blessed John Ruysbroeck, quoted by F. C. Happold, *Mysticism*, p. 293.
7. *Hadîth*.
8. Fakhruddîn 'Irâqî, p. 126.
9. Ibid., p. 88.

APPENDIX

1. Adapted from Irina Tweedie, unpublished lecture, Schwarzsee, Switzerland, 1989.

BIBLIOGRAPHY

'Abd al-Qâdir al-Jîlânî. *The Secret of Secrets*. Trans. Shaykh Tosun Bayrak. Cambridge: The Islamic Texts Society, 1992.

Addas, Claude. *Quest for the Red Sulphur, The Life of Ibn 'Arabî*. Cambridge: The Islamic Texts Society, 1994.

Al-Qushayrî. *Principles of Sufism*. Trans. B. R. Von Schlegell. Berkeley: Mizan Press, 1990.

'Arabî, Ibn. "Whoso Knoweth Himself..." Abingdon, Oxon: Beshara Publications, 1976.

'Attâr, Farîd ud-Dîn. *The Conference of the Birds*. Trans. C. S. Nott. London: Routledge & Kegan Paul, 1961.

——. Muslim Saints and Mystics. Trans. A. J. Arberry. London: Routledge & Kegan Paul, 1966.

Bennett, J. G. *Masters of Wisdom*. London: Turnstone Press, 1977.

Bhatnagar, R. S. *Dimensions of Classical Sufi Thought*. Delhi, India: Motilal Banarsidass, 1984.

The Bible, Authorized Version. London: 1611.

Castillejo, Irene de. *Knowing Woman*. New York: Harper Colophon, 1974.

Chittick, William C. *The Sufi Path of Love*. Albany: State University of New York Press, 1983.

——. *The Sufi Path of Knowledge*. Albany: State University of New York Press, 1989.

Cooper, J. C. *An Illustrated Encyclopedia of Traditional Symbols*. London: Thames and Hudson, 1978.

Corbin, Henry. *Creative Imagination in the Sufism of Ibn 'Arabî*. Princeton: Princeton University Press, 1969.

——. *The Man of Light in Iranian Sufism*. London: Shambhala Publications, 1978.

——. *Spiritual Body and Celestial Earth*. London: I. B. Taurus and Co., 1976.

Edinger, Edward. *The Anatomy of the Psyche*. La Salle: Open Court, 1985.

Eliot, T.S. *Collected Poems*. London: Faber and Faber, 1963.

Glassé, Cyril. *The Concise Encyclopedia of Islam*. San Francisco: Harper San Francisco, 1991.

Happold, F. C. *Mysticism*. Harmonsworth: Penguin Books, 1963.

Hillman, James. *Insearch: Psychology and Religion*. Dallas: Spring Publications, 1965.

'Irâqî, Fakhruddin. *Divine Flashes*. Trans. William C. Chittick and Peter Lamborn Wilson. New York: Paulist Press, 1982.

Jacobi, Jolande. *The Way of Individuation*. New York: Harcourt Brace and World, 1967.

Jensen, Ferne, ed. *C. G. Jung, Emma Jung, Toni Wolff: A Collection of Remembrances*. San Francisco: The Analytical Psychology Club of San Francisco, 1982.

Jung, C. G. *Collected Works*. London: Routledge & Kegan Paul.

—. *Psychology of the Transference*. London: Arc Paperbacks, 1983.

—. *Psychological Reflections*. London: Routledge & Kegan Paul, 1953.

—, ed. *Man and His Symbols*. London: Aldus Books, 1964.

Khan, Hazrat Inayat. *The Sufi Message of Hazrat Inayat Khan*, Vol. X. London: Barrie Jenkins, 1964.

The Koran. Trans. A. J. Arberry. New York: Macmillan, 1955.

The Koran. Trans. N. J. Dawood. London: Penguin Books, 1956.

Lao Tsu. *Tao Te Ching*. Trans. Gia-Fu Feng and Jane English. Aldershot, England: Wildwood House Ltd., 1973.

Lipski, Alexander. *Life and Teaching of Anandamayi Ma*. Delhi, India: Motilal Banarsidass, 1979.

Massignon, Louis. *The Passion of al-Hallâj*. Princeton: Princeton University Press, 1982.

Mitchell, Stephen, ed. *The Enlightened Heart*. New York: Harper & Row, 1989.

—, ed. *The Enlightened Mind*. New York: Harper Collins, 1991.

Nicholson, R. A. *Studies in Islamic Mysticism*. Cambridge: Cambridge University Press, 1921.

—. *The Mystics of Islam*. London: Arkana, 1989.

Nurbakhsh, Javad. *Sufi Symbolism*, Vol. I-IV. London: Khaniqahi-Nimatullahi Publications, 1984-1990.

O'Kane, John, trans. *The Secret of God's Mystical Oneness.* Costa Mesa, California: Mazda Publishers, 1992.

Rûmî. *One-Handed Basket Weaving.* Trans. Coleman Barks. Athens, Georgia: Maypop Books, 1991.

—. *Open Secret.* Trans. John Moyne and Coleman Barks. Putney, Vermont: Threshold Books, 1984.

—. *This Longing.* Trans. Coleman Barks and John Moyne. Putney, Vermont: Threshold Books, 1988.

—. *Love's Fire: Recreations of Rumi.* Trans. Andrew Harvey. Ithaca, New York: Meerama, 1989.

—. *Love is a Stranger.* Trans. Kabir Helminski. Putney, Vermont: Threshold Books, 1993.

—. *Rumi: Fragments, Ecstasies.* Trans. Daniel Liebert. Santa Fe, New Mexico: Source Books, 1981.

—. *Rûmî: Poet and Mystic.* Trans. R. A. Nicholson. London: George Allen and Unwin, 1950.

Scheeling, Andrew. *For Love of the Dark One: Songs of Mirabai.* Boston, Massachusetts: Shambhala, 1993.

Schimmel, Annemarie. *Mystical Dimensions of Islam.* Chapel Hill, North Carolina: University of North Carolina Press, 1975.

—. *The Triumphal Sun.* Albany: State University of New York Press, 1993.

Serrano, Miguel. *C. G. Jung and Hermann Hesse: A Record of Two Friendships.* London: Routledge & Kegan Paul, 1966.

Shâfi'î, Mohammad. *Freedom from the Self.* New York: Human Sciences Press, 1985.

Shakespeare, William. *The Tempest.* Ed. Frank Kermode. London: Methuen & Co. Ltd., 1954.

Thompson, Francis. *The Hound of Heaven.* London: Burns and Oates, 1915.

Tweedie, Irina. *Daughter of Fire: A Diary of a Spiritual Training with a Sufi Master.* Point Reyes, California: The Golden Sufi Center, 1986.

Underhill, Evelyn. *Mysticism.* New York: New American Library, 1974.

Upton, Charles. *Doorkeeper of the Heart: Versions of Râbi'a.* Putney, Vermont: Threshold Books, 1988.

Vaughan-Lee, Llewellyn. *The Lover and the Serpent: Dream-work within a Sufi Tradition*. Shaftesbury: Element Books, 1989. (Out of print).

—. *Catching the Thread: Sufism, Dreamwork and Jungian Psychology*. Point Reyes, California: The Golden Sufi Center, 1998.

—. *The Bond with the Beloved: The Mystical Relationship of the Lover and the Beloved*. Point Reyes, California: The Golden Sufi Center, 1993.

—. *In the Company of Friends: Dreamwork within a Sufi Group*. Point Reyes, California: The Golden Sufi Center, 1994.

Vitray-Meyerovitch, Eva de. *Rûmî and Sufism*. Sausalito, California: The Post-Apollo Press, 1987.

Wilson, Peter Lamborn and Pourjavady, Nasrollah. *The Drunken Universe*. Grand Rapids: Phanes Press, 1987.

Yeats, W. B., trans. (with Shree Purohit Swami). *The Ten Principal Upanishads*. London: Faber and Faber, 1937.

Zweig, Connie and Abrams, Jeremiah, ed. *Meeting the Shadow*. Los Angeles: Jeremy P. Tarcher, 1990.

INDEX

W

wahdat al-wujûd (unity of being) xvi, xviii

wine xiii, 7, 11, 81, 130, 132, 139

witch 52, 59, 158

Y

Yahyâ ibn Ma'âdh (d. 871-2) 132n

Z

Zen 35, 92, 126, 129

ACKNOWLEDGMENTS

For permission to use copyrighted material, the author gratefully wishes to acknowledge: Daniel Liebert, for permission to quote from *Rumi: Fragments, Ecstasies,* translated by Daniel Liebert; Maypop Books, for permission to quote from *One-Handed Basket Weaving,* translated by Coleman Barks; Mazda Publishers, for permission to quote from *The Secrets of God's Mystical Oneness,* by Ebn-e Monawwar, translated by John O'Kane; Meeramma Publications, for permission to quote from *Love's Fire,* by Andrew Harvey; Mizan Press for permission to quote from *Principles of Sufism,* by al-Qushayrî, translated by B.R. Von Schlegell, permission conveyed through Copyright Clearance Center, Inc.; Octagon Press for permission to quote from "The Abode of Spring" by Jami, translated by David Pendlebury, from *Four Sufi Classics;* Paulist Press, for permission to quote from *Fakhruddin 'Iraqi: Divine Flashes,* by Fakhruddin 'Irâqî, translation and introduction by William C. Chittick and Peter Lamborn Wilson, © 1982; Threshold Books (www.sufism.org) for permission to quote from *This Longing* and *Open Secret,* translated by John Moyne and Coleman Barks, and *Doorkeeper of the Heart,* translated by Charles Upton.

LLEWELLYN VAUGHAN-LEE, Ph.D., is a Sufi teacher in the Naqshbandiyya-Mujaddidiyya Sufi Order. Born in London in 1953, he has followed the Naqshbandi Sufi path since he was nineteen. In 1991 he became the successor of Irina Tweedie, author of *Daughter of Fire: A Diary of a Spiritual Training with a Sufi Master.* He then moved to Northern California and founded The Golden Sufi Center (goldensufi.org). Author of several books, he has specialized in the area of dreamwork, integrating the ancient Sufi approach to dreams with the insights of Jungian Psychology. Since the year 2000 the focus of his writing and teaching has been on spiritual responsibility in our present time of transition, the awakening global consciousness of oneness, and spiritual ecology (workingwithoneness.org) He was featured in the TV series *Global Spirit,* and interviewed by Oprah Winfrey as part of her *Super Soul Sunday* series.

THE GOLDEN SUFI CENTER is a California Religious 501 (c) 3 Nonprofit Corporation dedicated to making the teachings of the Naqshbandi Sufi Path available to all seekers. For further information about activities and publications, please contact:

The Golden Sufi Center
P.O. Box 456
Point Reyes, California 94956
tel: (415) 663-0100 · *fax:* (415) 663-0103
www.goldensufi.org